Radical Obedience

The Secrets Of Surrender And A Real
Lived-Out Love For God

By Toyin Crandell

JEREMIAH HOUSE PUBLISHING
Toronto, Ontario

Published in Toronto, Ontario, Canada by Jeremiah House Publishing.

Unless otherwise noted, all scripture quotations are from the New American Standard Bible, copyright 1960, 1962, 1963, 1968, 1971, 1972, 1973, 1975, 1977 by the Lockman Foundation. Used by permission.

Scripture quotations marked NKJV are taken from the New King James Version. Copyright 1982 by Thomas Nelson, Inc. Used by permission.

Scriptures marked ESV are taken from the Holy Bible, English Standard Version (ESV): Copyright© 2001 by Crossway, of Good News Publishers. Used by permission.

Any italicization or words in brackets added to scripture quotations are the author's addition for emphasis or clarity.

Organizations, churches, pastors and small group leaders can receive special discounts when purchasing this book and other Jeremiah House Publishing resources. For more information, please email info@jeremiahhousepublishing.com

Crandell, Toyin, 1988-, author
Radical Obedience: The Secrets Of Surrender And A Real Lived-Out Love For God / Toyin Crandell.

ISBN 978-1-989066-07-2 (Paperback)
ISBN 978-1-989066-10-2 (Hardcover)
ISBN 978-1-989066-09-6 (Audiobook)
ISBN 978-1-989066-08-9 (Electronic)

Religion & Spirituality: Christian Living: Leadership & Mentoring
Religion & Spirituality: Christian Living: Calling & Vocation

Printed In Canada

TABLE OF CONTENTS

DEDICATION

I dedicate this book to my children —
Maranatha, Nehemiah and Esperanza.
You are my motivation for completing and releasing this book.
If I have taught you anything with my life, it doesn't compare
with my desire that you understand this:

Jesus is worthy of your Yes. He is worthy of your ALL.
Everything this world has to offer you pales in comparison to
the knowledge that you walk with Him, hear His voice and
follow closely.
That is my highest prayer for you.

PRELUDE

You may have heard stories of people who obeyed God by travelling to the unknown corners of the earth to share the gospel. People who started large crusade movements, changing millions of lives for Christ. You may even have heard of those who pastor churches the size of cities.

But this book, will take you on the journey of obedience to God, right where you are. It will charge, convict and equip you to live in obedience to Jesus, wherever you are right now, whether that's in North or South America, Africa, Asia, Australia or elsewhere.

This book itself is evidence of learned obedience.

You see, while I have walked with God for over a decade in joyful obedience, I felt that I did not know enough to write on the subject of obeying God. In fact, when He charged me to do so, I chickened out. I had always done my best to do most of the things He asked, but this one challenged me to my core.

And it's not because I didn't want to write it.

The subject was too dear to my heart. Now, all of a sudden, the desire to be perfect in each word, each stroke of my pen, to not misspeak or mislead, led me to a standstill.

I'd written a best-selling book *"Money Mindset SHIFT. Church Edition: The Top 9 Myths That Keep Christians Stuck Financially and How To Get Unstuck, Live Debt Free and Build Wealth!"* I had ghostwritten best-sellers for other authors. I even was the CEO of a self-publishing company, and I still couldn't imagine where to start with this book.

So, I sat on the idea for 6 years. It wasn't until I felt the Holy Spirit warn me that I would miss a major assignment for my life if this book was not completed. That pushed me to take courage and begin the process.

However, I made another error.

I'm sure you're wondering why I would start a book about obedience with the mistakes I made. But I promise you, stick with me and you'll understand.

Now, back to my error. When I finally decided to start this book, instead of writing it myself, I chose to invest money into getting it ghostwritten. It was so precious to me that I didn't want to say anything the wrong way. **However, what I was really saying was that this message was too important for my voice, as is.** I figured there was a professional out there that could make it sound the way it needed to for the largest viewership possible. So as soon as I could, I saved up about $65,000 USD to get the best of the best.

When God Hinders You

We kicked off the project and everything that could happen, did. This was not the fault of the company I hired. We moved homes, had a baby, ran for political office as a family, and my company had massive moments of transition and growth. Now, this book that was supposed to be written within 5 - 6 months, started to take longer and longer. Before I knew it, 2 years had gone by.

Something else was happening with the book. I stopped feeling like it carried the anointing of the message God had given me, and I didn't understand why. I would hesitate each time I worked on the book and it felt like writer's block. I would procrastinate on our writing meetings. And even when I sat with the book, it felt like I had nothing to say. I couldn't work on it. I didn't know what to do. I had no clue why I had lost all zeal for this message that I KNEW was a foundational part of what God had called me to do.

Technically, at this point, the book was written —all 450 pages of it,120,000 words. It was long, it was bulky, and it was not anointed.

At first, I figured I simply needed to cut it down to 300 pages and about 80,000 words, but I had no idea where to start and what to cut or keep. I chalked it up to an editing problem. But I had edited numerous other books. Why was this so different?

I thought it was a time management problem. I tried scheduling accountability sessions. I tried time blocking for focus. As a matter of fact, I already knew how to manage my time as a homeschooling mom of 2 with a multi-million dollar organization. Time management couldn't be the issue. This felt deeper than that. So what was it?!

I posted about the book, getting insight from hundreds of people on the cover, the title and everything else. But I couldn't bring myself to move forward with any of it.

Two years had passed and this book still wasn't done. I finally emailed the company to let them know I was ready to make it my full-time focus, rain or shine. I would push through, even if it didn't feel like there was a grace on it.

And then I got the news. This company that was world renown (not an exaggeration) for publishing international New York Times and Wall Street Journal Bestsellers had gone bankrupt — with my book in their cue.

This meant that everyone I was working with had been fired. My book was immediately halted. I would need to pay an exorbitant amount in order to continue working with the new owners of the company.

In other words, that was the end.

But it couldn't be.

A Fresh Start

So I took full ownership of the journey, again.

I made the decision that the book would be completely written before the end of that year.

I prayed and asked God for help and mercy. I wanted to know what had been holding this book back, and exactly what I needed to do to finish it.

In this place of desperate prayer, He led me to an event where I had the opportunity to spend time with John Maxwell's writer – Charlie Wetzel, and his wife, Stephanie. Wetzel partnered with Maxwell to write over 100 books in the last 30 years.

They spent 10 minutes speaking to me about this book on a bus ride to an event. They helped me to see two things: first, that the message of the book had changed from its original audience and intent, to now trying to speak to those it was not intended for. Secondly, that trying to please the experts I had partnered with had watered down the message, and caused me to lose the fire I initially had. They suggested I remember my first audience, and my first message, and cut out whatever was inserted outside of that place of inspiration.

A Fire Rekindled

I got home from that event and finally heard God speak about the book.

He said, "Rewrite the book."

Now technically, I had heard God say that numerous times over the 2 years. But I didn't believe He actually meant to scrap all the work we had already done.

All the money I had invested.

And rewrite the book from scratch.

That same week, I saw a quote I had posted on social media 7 years ago come back up on my feed; thank you Facebook Memories. It was a quote from Bill Bright. It said, "When God gives a man a vision, he is never to delegate it to someone else." And all of a sudden it clicked.

When God gave me this vision, He asked me to write from the intimate place of my journey of obedience — a journey which has caused thousands of people to want to love Jesus and passionately obey Him. I cared so much about it sounding the "right" way, that I decided to put money where my voice was supposed to be and delegated the task. While delegation is great, in this case, God did not tell me to give it to a company to write. I did that because of fear.

I was afraid that if I told this story myself, it would not reach the people who are praying for a breakthrough in this area. I was convinced that the only way this book could be a potential New York Times Bestseller was if a better writer took the lead.

This fear and insecurity caused me to give my voice away.

I repented immediately.

I picked up my laptop, looked at the tab that had been open on my computer for years–you know those "I'll get to this soon" tabs–with the 120,000 word document I had been slaving over for years – and I closed it.

I opened up a blank page and allowed Jesus to speak to and through me, to you.

So welcome. Come in and take a seat. If you are ready to experience a life of faith, love and the type of obedience that proves that the God of the Bible is still alive, then this book will be one you read again, year after year. Your life can display the type of obedience that causes your grandchildren or friends around the Thanksgiving table, to ask for more stories about your history in pursuing Jesus, and seeing Him show up in your everyday setting.

This book will teach you:

- How to make mistakes, dust yourself off and keep running the race of faith, over and over again.
- How to receive the love of God even when you feel the least deserving of it.
- How to walk with clarity of mind and purpose even when things are going crazy around you.
- How to win BIG at the things God calls you to do.
- How to know that you are living a life of radical obedience, motivated by love instead of fear.

This book will teach you how to trust that the One who has called you, is faithful to assist you in doing what He has called you to do. Share this book with those who pursue the Lord with you. The sharper your community is in obedience, the sharper you become.

PART

1

THE FOUNDATION
FOR OBEDIENCE

Chapter 1:

WHY OBEDIENCE MATTERS

Obedience, in my experience, is one of the most discussed topics in Christian circles. We have full-length Bible studies and sermons on it. We can share dissertations, with verse-by-verse recitation.

And it feels absolutely glorious – until you encounter something you don't want to do, or feel stuck because you aren't clear about what God wants you to do in a certain season. Or imagine that, you finally step out in what you feel God said to do, and you're met with huge backlash and criticism. Even worse, you step out and you are met with nothing. No big positive, no big negative, just nothing.

Obedience is an "easier said than done" conversation.

Many of us start our walk with God in a place of absolute surrender; *"God have every part of me!"* We sing the songs and pray the prayers, but over the years, a disillusionment sets in. We faced disappointments. We felt the pushback. For some of us, we have gotten distracted. We're comfortable, complacent, and we've settled into the Western "Sunday-to-Sunday" version of

3

Christianity we swore to never settle for.

Meanwhile, your heart is crying out *there has to be more.*

And God calls you to this *more* because obedience is not an option. It is part of the foundation of a healthy, honest relationship with Him.

Obedience is part of the foundation of a healthy, honest relationship with God.

God's Love Language

In John 15, Jesus gives us a beautiful picture of relationship with Him: "I am the vine, you are the branches; he who abides in Me and I in him, he bears much fruit, for apart from Me you can do nothing." It is an image of connection, love, and fruitfulness—one where we are desperately dependent on God and we grow in His love because we are intertwined with Him. It's a beautiful display of His perspective of our relationship. Soon after, Jesus gives the disciples the secret to His heart. He sums up what it means to show *Him* friendship and love. He says, "*...You are My friends **if** you do what I command you.*"[1]

> ***Obedience is God's love language.***

You may have heard about the five Love Languages by Gary Chapman. They are a list of ways we receive and express love to one another. They include things like physical touch, quality time, words of affirmation, etc. Many of us want to show God

---

[1] John 15:14

that we love Him in our way by singing worship songs, attending a church, reading the Bible and so on. Yet, Jesus made God's love language clear and most people miss it.

It's radical obedience.

This is emphasized throughout scripture:

- "My little children, let us not love in word or in tongue, but *in action and in truth.*"[2]
- "*If* you love me, you *will* keep my commandments."[3]
- "But *be doers of the word*, and not hearers only, deceiving yourselves."[4]
- "And Samuel said, "Has the Lord as great delight in burnt offerings and sacrifices, as in obeying the voice of the Lord? Behold, *to obey is better than sacrifice*, and to listen than the fat of rams."[5]
- "Jesus answered him, "If anyone loves me, *he will keep my word*, and my Father will love him, and we will come to him and make our home with him."[6]
- "Why do you call me 'Lord, Lord,' *and not do what I tell you?*"[7]

There's a difference between simply reading the Bible and praying, versus having a life surrendered to His leadership.

Once, while driving downtown to minister, my team and I

---

[2] 1 John 3:18

[3] John 14:15

[4] James 1:22

[5] 1 Samuel 15:22

[6] John 14:23

[7] Luke 6:46

started talking about the fact that we sing so many songs to God that we aren't willing to back up. We sing words like, "Take everything away till all I have is you," or, "I wanna be tried by fire, purified. You take whatever you desire, Lord here's my life," but don't really mean it. We don't want to be tried by His purifying fire. We don't want him to take everything away. We want our comfort and Jesus in a box with a neatly tied bow on top.

We were so marked by this conversation that we started to pray and ask God for the grace to live out the song lyrics we sing. Being musicians, we ended up singing the prayer and it turned into a song called, "In the Name of Love," which is on our album *Living out Love*. In it, we sing these words:

"Give us the grace to live out what we sing, living only for our King, that You would grant the strength to carry Your glory. Love is not just words, but it's action and deeds. This is what You said, that if we love You we would cleave, to Your commands, to Your direction.

We'll follow Your plan, we'll go the distance."

This is God's love language.

It's our *actions* that tell God, "I hear you, Abba (this is the Aramaic word for father, and another name I use interchangeably with God). I'm with you. I love you. I want more of you. So I choose to do what You're telling me to do."

Throughout the Bible, God says in different forms, "I love you and I have given much for you. Will you love me in return?"

And when Abraham, Moses, Mary, or Peter responded, "Yes, Lord—I love you"—the Lord's response was almost always a direction to *act:*

- "Take now your son, your only son, whom you love, Isaac, and go to the land of Moriah, and offer him there as a burnt offering on one of the mountains of which I will tell you."[8]
- "Feed my sheep"[9].
- "Now the Lord spoke to Moses in the Wilderness of Sinai…Thus the children of Israel did; according to all that the Lord commanded Moses, so they did.[10]

And it's reciprocal. When Moses requested to see God's face, He responded, "I will also *do* this thing of which you have spoken; for you have found favor in My sight and I have known you by name."[11] God said to Moses, I will do what you've asked because I love you.

Obedience is Better Than Sacrifice

Obedience matters to God; Doing what He says, when He says to do it. When King Saul was given a commission to destroy the Amalekites completely, this was his assignment:

"This is what the Lord of armies says: 'I will punish Amalek for what he did to Israel, in that he obstructed him on the way

---

[8] Abraham, Genesis 22:2

[9] Peter, Luke 6:46

[10] Moses, Numbers 1:1, 54; Numbers 2:1, 34; 3:5, 11, 14, 51

[11] Exodus 33:17

while he was coming up from Egypt. *Now go and strike Amalek and completely destroy everything that he has, and do not spare him*; but put to death both man and woman, child and infant, ox and sheep, camel and donkey.'"[12]

God was very clear in His directive to Saul, yet, Saul decided to follow some but not all of His direction. He went 90% of the way; and incomplete obedience *is* disobedience.

"Then Saul defeated the Amalekites, from Havilah going toward Shur, which is east of Egypt. He captured Agag the king of the Amalekites alive, and completely destroyed all the people with the edge of the sword. But Saul and the people spared Agag and the best of the sheep, the oxen, the more valuable animals, the lambs, and everything that was good, and were unwilling to destroy them completely;" [13]

It's easy to judge Saul and think, "How could he miss something so simple, so clear. I would never have done that." But do most of us even do the 90%? Some of us have ignored the message and direction God has been giving for years and our ears have grown dull of hearing. This is the sober state for many believers.

So while I read this story about Saul, I am often asking the Lord to search my heart and show me anyway I am doing 90% of what He is saying, and holding back out of fear or because I prefer the opinion of others.

---

[12] 1 Samuel 15:3

[13] 1 Samuel 15:7-9

God said to the prophet Samuel, "I regret that I have made Saul king, because he has turned back from following Me and *has not carried out My commands.*" Even though Saul had done 90% of what God said to do.

In fact, God shares with us that He would rather have our obedience than our offerings of money or songs. If we want to have a true history with God, we need to be submitted to His perspective on how we speak, act, post online, and joke around. We need to be willing to change into His image and have our hearts open to do what He says, even when we don't feel like it.

> **We must love God on His terms, not ours.**

I won't sugar-coat it. Radical obedience takes a deeper motivation than simply wanting to check the boxes. You can check boxes on church attendance, but not on a major life transition God may call you to do. Those take a deeper level of trust. And to be honest, I did not do well with or enjoy this for the first few years I tried to obey God fully. So how on earth did I get to a place where I can write on the topic of *joyful, radical obedience*?

The Start

You see, I grew up loving the idea of obedience, in theory. Growing up in a Nigerian home, we were taught to obey our parents, listen to your teachers and do as you are told. I tried to follow the rules and didn't think about it much. I wasn't a rebellious child toward my parents, but one area where my rebellion would show up was in my heart towards God. It wasn't an external thing. Growing up in the church and knowing most of the "rules", I did everything I could tell was right when people were looking. However, for the first couple of decades of my life, as much as I enjoyed the idea of obedience, I couldn't do it. I wanted to live in a way that honoured my earthly father's God, but my flesh simply wanted, and did, other things.

The more I tried, the more I failed. I went to the altar multiple times at my church and at youth events, laying down habits or friendships that I knew God wanted me to let go of.

A part of me wanted to live this godly lifestyle, while the other part thought it would be a prison sentence or the most boring life I could ever commit to. Before I knew what God was like, I thought He was as boring as paper. I thought He was this distant, menacing entity who monitored our activities only to check whether or not we deserved to make it to heaven. I came from a very prayerful church that saw a lot of answered prayers, but I figured that was just part of His function, not proof of His emotion or involvement in our lives.

In those years, I tried to read the Bible but 5 minutes in, my mind would wonder about what was cooking for dinner. When my dad would call the family to pray every morning, it was the biggest struggle to stay awake and care about what we were doing. Even when I would pay attention or contribute, it was so that I wasn't told to stand up because I fell asleep. It certainly was not because I was riveted by the man, Christ Jesus, that we were talking about.

Almost Arrested For Christ

Yet, six years later, I nearly got arrested for passionately leading worship on one of the busiest streets in Toronto, because I couldn't shut up about how real and amazing Jesus is. Crazy.

I was working with a team to serve food to the homeless, organize street Bible studies, and perform music. We had read an article about that period of time being termed "the year of the gun," as the city was experiencing some of the highest gun-murder rates it had ever seen. In fact, there had been a shoot-out on that very corner. People didn't linger there; they would walk through as fast as possible. You could feel the fear and distrust in the atmosphere, and we wanted to fight that darkness by bringing the joy of the Lord.

We sang about how good God is and how much He loved us. Crowds would stand around to listen and we would share the gospel in between songs. One afternoon, a bylaw officer interrupted our flag-waving, singing, and djembe-playing. He said, "You guys can't do this here."

Beside us, buskers were dancing and playing music in order to ask for money (which we weren't doing). My heart started to pound, respectfully and nervously, I said, "We're not collecting money. We have the right to be here, we're praising God."

The bylaw officer pointed across the street to a group of police officers nearby. "If you're not going to pack up your stuff and get out, I'll have them come and help you do it. And you will all be arrested." We had been doing this for a few weeks with no issues, and I had never been challenged about sharing the gospel until this moment. Everything in me wanted to say to my team, "Okay, let's wrap this up and go

11

read our Bibles at home." But these people getting to know the love and reality of Jesus Christ was worth more to me than the fear I felt.

At this point, God wasn't boring. I was completely sold out to Him. He could tell me to do anything, and I would do it, even if it was difficult, even if it was scary. I was so in love and so grateful for His goodness to me! I wanted everyone with a false idea of God—like the one I'd had—to understand what I did: that He is real and He is good.

I looked around. Even while I had stepped aside to talk to the officer, the crowd hadn't dispersed. They were listening intently to the rest of the team, singing and clapping along. Some were having one-on-one conversations with different team members to learn more about the gospel.

So, through my fear, I said to the officer, "Okay. Go ahead and do whatever you want. I'm in charge, so if you're going to arrest anyone, you can just take me."

He crossed the street, and I got back on my djembe, joined the team and started singing: "Freeedooom! No more shackles, no more chains, no more bondage. I am free!"[14]

The man spoke with the other officers across the street and started walking back toward us. My heart raced as I braced myself for the worst, asking myself, "Are you really ready to go to jail for the gospel?" I didn't know this was possible in Canada.

I looked at him ready for a challenge, but his next words shocked all of us. He said, "You know what? I really appreciate

---

[14] Song: "Freedom, No More Shackles" by Eddie James

what you guys are doing. Keep going. In fact, you can come here anytime you want." I couldn't imagine what his conversation with the other officers could have been, but his change of heart was a true miracle. With huge relief, I said, "Thank you so much!" Then, I pushed it, "Do you mind if we pray for you?" I asked.

He responded, "Sure, go ahead."

So we prayed for him and his family. I still remember his name, David. Then we went back to singing and sharing the gospel through art, music, and spoken word on that street corner every Monday and Wednesday. And we continued to do it that summer, the following, and the summer after that.

Motivation That Lasts

Choosing to say no to your flesh and trust God enough to do the unthinkable can be difficult. I won't sugar-coat it. But in order for the stories I share in this book to make sense, you need to understand why I kept pursuing this place of free and full obedience to Abba with everything in me. Especially when I was coming from a place of not caring about Him almost at all.

The truth is if you don't have a strong enough reason for obeying God you won't do it. It's that simple. You'll talk about it. You'll have powerful Bible studies on the topic. You'll tell everyone else how good it is to obey God. You will sing songs and record prophecies about what you will do one day. But you will not step out of that boat in an attempt to walk on water unless you personally have an unquestionable reason to do so.

Even when I was radically changed, and committed to obeying Christ's leadership for the first few years, I often did it reluctantly. Each task took me ages to follow through on. If you imagined me as Peter, when Jesus called him to walk on the water, I would often put one foot out, bring it back, try again, yell at how cold the water was, retreat again, but finally, by dawn, have started holding his hands and stepping out.

It wasn't until some years later that God changed my perspective. He showed me the genuine, thorough overflowing joy that comes out of living this life of obedience, where it isn't you that lives, but Christ living in you. Some people told me in those first few years of pursuing the Lord, "Why are you so much? Are you the first person to become a Christian? Following Jesus doesn't require all of this, you don't have to do all this."

I was committed to obey Him even though my flesh didn't agree with what He said many times. What was my motivation to overcome my flesh and learn to trust Him? Why did I care so much that I obeyed Him when I didn't feel like it? What motivated my commitment to Jesus' leadership, even while I was still learning how to trust Him practically, was knowing how much He loved me.

He loved me more than any other person on the planet did, and does. I couldn't get away from that type of love. I wanted to be wherever He was. So if being where He was meant laying on the floor in my bedroom, weeping and praying to the Father, that's where I wanted to be. If that meant being in the studio singing about God's love, that's where I wanted to be. If that meant speaking on stages and sharing wisdom that would transform lives radically, both financially and holistically, I wanted to be there. If that meant being spit on by passers-by while talking about God's love, that's where I wanted to be. If that meant being in Cambodia's slums, sitting in tin huts and singing in Khmer about "How He loves us" with prostitutes, that's where I wanted to be. If being where He was meant sitting on the floor doing laundry with a 7, 4 and 1 year old crawling all over, while praying in the Spirit, I wanted to be there. If that meant leading a multimillion dollar company and transforming tens of thousands of lives, I would be there as well.

All I wanted was to be where He was.

So how did I go from thinking God was the most boring entity to wanting to be the white to His rice? The mac to His cheese? The peanut to His butter?

My friend, sit down, grab your coffee and let me gist you (Nigerian slang for "tell you the story").

Chapter 2

FROM BORED TO BRANDED

But God demonstrates His own love toward us, in that while we
were still sinners, Christ died for us.
Romans 5:8

Like I said earlier, I grew up in the church and lived what seemed like a picture perfect life. Now, let me *ahem* clarify. I lived a thoroughly hypocritical life. To the majority of people in my church and those I would minister to, I was singing and "ministering" out of my talent before I even knew who God was.

In fact, back then I *really did* think I knew Jesus. I thought I had given Him my life because I said the "sinner's prayer" multiple times, and went up to the altar to "give my life to God" over and over again. But I had never been regenerated by His Spirit. I had never actually, truly been converted into a follower of Jesus Christ.

So what did that mean? I created structures to present a front to everyone around me of being holy and Christ-like, even though there was no real power to live that way.

At that time, I was in a romantic relationship that was completely outside of the will of God. How did I know this? We were consistently in sexual sin[15].

I couldn't stop my flesh from sinning. Sin ruled over me. I lied compulsively. I would tell my parents I was going to the library after a full day of studies at school, when I spent the entire day sitting in my boyfriend's apartment cooking and playing wife. I had an entire life that they knew nothing about. I rented an apartment for him, bought him a car and even had a secret dog. Reflecting on that time, I ask myself, "Why keep the dog a secret? Who does that? This girl. The one who was trying to "live her best life".

I thought I had everyone fooled.

What makes this even worse was that we were ministering together. We would sing in the choir on Sunday morning, sin in the afternoon, and repent on Sunday night. Yet, in lying to myself so much about what I was doing and how I was living, I believed my own lie. I really thought that I was saved, Christian and going to heaven.

Even though I would weep over and over, feeling stuck in this situation, I would then console myself with the words he said. "Toyin, we just need to repent and keep trying to follow God. This is why we are Christians. This is why we need the

---

[15] Some people wait to know if a relationship is God's will by prayer, fasting, seeking Him, asking people around them, all the while living in sexual sin with that person. Regarding compromising (sexual) relationships: God made His will clear. 1 Thessalonians 4:3 says, "For this is the will of God, your sanctification: that you should abstain from sexual immorality". Address that first, then you will be able to hear clearly whether that person is for you.

blood of Jesus. The church wasn't made for perfect people. We're imperfect and that's okay."

I ate up those words like candy to console and silence my conscience which gradually shut down until I stopped caring about my sinful lifestyle. I just lived it, believing that God was disconnected from me and all that was happening. I believed that He saw only my Sunday performances and was pleased with it because people were being "ministered to" through His anointing on my life.

Her Witness

Now, there was one particular woman who arrested my attention. She genuinely seemed to love God and she would talk about Him like they had a relationship all the time. She would say things like, "God led me to do this, and He had me do that," or, "I was praying today and God said..." etc. I was intrigued by the relationship she had with God and wanted that for myself. Up until that point, I read about Him in the Bible, sang about Him every day in our family's devotional time and on Sundays, and said rehearsed prayers, copied from what I had heard others pray. But deep down, I knew I was struggling and needed this type of relationship with God, the Father.

So I prayed and asked God, "If you're real, if you can be my Father, and direct me like you direct this woman, please show yourself to me." And nothing changed. No angels surrounded me with supernatural encounters. In fact, every time I picked up the Bible, it was the same story. I would get bored by the 5th verse and if I tried to pray, I'd be asleep within 2 minutes of starting. It was horrible.

After some time trying, deflated and disappointed in myself, I figured that God really was distant and that I would meet Him on the day I died. He would see all the "good" I did –community work, service in church, and my rehearsed prayers–-and receive me into heaven.

I believed my own lies in the life I had curated for others to see.

He Came To Me

Eventually, I gave up and forgot about my fervent desire to really know God. However, one particular day, something changed. I was cleaning my room and had my music player on. It was going from song to song, and at one point it got to a sermon by Paul Washer, a Christian missionary. I paused my laundry sorting, wondering if I should skip the sermon. I decided against it, and to be honest, I just didn't care either way.

Paul started to speak about the holiness of God. My first thought was, "Yea, yea, I've heard this before. We all know God is holy". He expounded on just how separate from sin God was, how impossible it was for men to know God while in our sinful state. He spoke about how impossible it was for us to get to heaven outside of the sacrifice that Christ made on the cross. After much stressing of the point, I agreed that, yes, God is holy and there is no sin in Him[16].

---

[16] 1 John 3:5 (NLT) says, "And you know that Jesus came to take away our sins, and there is no sin in him." For additional reading, please see 1 John 1:5 (NLT) and Psalm 92:15.

Then he began to speak about Romans 3:23, "For all have sinned and fall short of the glory of God." I agreed with this as well. The slight distinction was that "all have sinned" always meant *other people* in my mind. I could tell someone, "all have sinned and fall short of the glory of God," but what I really meant was, *you* have sinned and fall short of the glory of God. I was so stuck in my lies that I really didn't think of myself as a sinner, even though you can clearly see the mess I was in.

Romans 3:10-12 (ESV) says, "None is righteous, no, not one; no one understands; no one seeks for God. All have turned aside; together they have become worthless; no one does good, not even one."[17]

As he spoke of "all" sinning and how no one is good before God's eyes based on our own merit, I was casually nodding along while sorting my clothes, until he made a point that stopped me in my tracks. He said, "If you are living your life and it is not for the glory of God, you have sinned." I told myself in that moment, "Yes I do live for the glory of God. Look at all I do."

Then he gave an illustration. He asked two men on the front row what their names were. Let's say, Joey and Mike. He asked if either had met him before and both said no. Then he said, "Let's say I do something nice for Joey. He thanks me and I tell him, 'Oh, that's totally alright, I did it for Mike over here. It was all for him." He continued. "Could that be true? Could I attribute what I had done for Joey to my relationship with this man I know nothing about?" The logical answer was no.

I paused my cleaning.

---

[17] For additional reading, see Psalm 14:1-3 (ESV).

In that moment, I realized it was impossible to live or do anything for someone you don't know or have a real relationship with. And in this case, if your life isn't being lived for God, then it is being lived for yourself. Whether I wanted to admit it or not, I realized that if God is not the center of your existence, then you have set yourself up as your god, and that is sin.

I was doing a lot of "good" things and people would often say, thank you for my service. Here in North America, when we say thank you, the normal response is "you're welcome". However, in Nigerian culture, when someone says thank you, the response is, "Thank God." I said, "thank God," or, "glory be to God," all the time, and I had convinced myself that I was doing these things for God.

But I knew that I did not have a genuine relationship with God, at all. How could I say I had been living for God when I had no real relationship with Him? Even in the choir, I would sing songs with emotion and feeling, but not because I was singing to Him; the song was supposed to be performed expressively.

I started to think, "If I haven't been living for God, who am I living for?" The next thought followed quickly. "I've been living for me. I've been living for the thank yous. I have been living to hear, "Toyin is good." I have been dressing, singing, lying, pretending all for my good; it hasn't been for God at all." Then finally it hit me "*I* am not living for the glory of God. This means *I* have fallen short of the glory of God. Which means *I* am a sinner."

Even more, it hit me that going to church, checking the boxes, and doing "Christian things" did not mean I was living for the glory of God.

As soon as I had the thought, "I am a sinner," it was as if God stepped into the room. Everything around me changed. I was trembling. The air was electric. An image of a list came to my mind. It was as though God started to list out the many ways I had been sinning.

The first thing on the list was lies.

Lies

He showed me that I had built my entire life on lies.

Looking back, I used to lie so much that some people at my high school nicknamed me "Crafty". They would call me when they had done something wrong and were about to get in trouble with their parents. I would help them create a lie that would be accepted by their parents and get them off the hook. I would lie even when I didn't need to. It just seemed to flow out of me.

Now in our generation, we treat lies as such a small thing, but in that moment, I felt the hatred that God had for even the smallest lie.

Proverbs 6:16-19 (ESV) says, "There are six things that the Lord hates, seven that are an abomination to him: haughty eyes, *a lying tongue,* and hands that shed innocent blood, a heart that devises wicked plans, feet that make haste to run to evil, *a false witness who breathes out lies,* and one who sows discord among brothers."

Notice that out of the seven things that are an abomination to Him lies[18] are listed twice! However, the scripture that stayed on my mind was, John 8:44 (ESV):

"You are of your father the devil, and your will is to do your father's desires. He was a murderer from the beginning, and has nothing to do with the truth, because there is no truth in him. When he lies, he speaks out of his own character, for he is a liar and the father of lies."

It reminded me that the devil himself is the father of all lies. God showed me that my inspiration for lies had never been from Him. In fact, they were against everything He stood for. He showed me that my pride in being called crafty and being a go-to person for helping others lie was completely against His heart.

What had once been such a casual thing –to lie to my parents constantly–weighed heavily against me and He saw each and every one.

The next thing on the list was sexual immorality.

Sexual Immorality

He opened my eyes to see how wicked I had been in choosing my flesh, my desires and a man, over Him; knowing that what I was doing was wrong, but going along with it because it felt good, and no one knew about it.

He continued down the list and pointed out so many things I did consistently against His holy nature. Then he came to the last item on the list, and the floor felt as if it collapsed under me. The word was murder.

---

[18] For further reading on lies, please see Proverbs 19:9 (ESV), Proverbs 12:22 (ESV), and Psalm 101:7 (ESV).

Murder

No one knew about my two abortions. My boyfriend knew about the first one (he'd demanded that I do it), but not the second at the end of our relationship. I had made a commitment to myself that no one else would ever know about them. It was my secret. And because I'd hidden them from everyone, I managed to convince myself that they had never happened.

But God was there.

God spoke gently, "Toyin, those were my children. They were real children, they had destinies, and I had a plan for them." I crumpled on the floor in the middle of my stack of unfolded clothes and wept. The weight of what I had done, and what I was still doing, crushed me.

My deepest secrets were laid out in front of a Holy God. I knew that God saw every single thing I had done against His will, even the ones I tried to hide from myself and forgot about. I knew that without His mercy, every single one of my sins would weigh against me on the day of judgment.

I knew that no "good deed" could make up for all of my sins. I couldn't bribe Him. He knew everything. I was now convinced that I was the worst sinner I knew. I am not saying this to be pious, I mean it. When I saw the full extent of my selfishness, I was ashamed. I wanted to disappear, but I also *didn't* want to die and have to face His judgment. I didn't even know where to run to.

My face was covered in a mixture of tears and snot and in the midst of that hot mess, I heard God say, "Toyin, I love you." It didn't make any sense. I thought, "No, you can't love me. I just heard a sermon about how sinless and holy God is. Someone like that could not love someone like me. How can you love someone like me? If my own family, and my closest friends knew all that you know about me, they would not want to eat from the same plate as me."

He responded, "*This* is the gospel Toyin, this is what I sent my Son, Jesus to die for. He died on the cross so that you can be fully forgiven for every single one of these sins and if you accept Him into your heart. If you will give your life to Me, you will be completely free. You will be clean."

I was floored. I cried like I had never cried before in my life. I knew what God was saying was true. I realized that I had never before actually known what His grace meant because I had never known what my sin looked like. I broke down and gave Him everything. It sounded something like, "Lord I believe you, I can't believe you would love me like this. Thank you, I give You my life. You have me." As I said that I felt His pure, clean love wash right over me. I knew I was clean. I saw the long list of sins fade away.

Transformed

I had a blank slate. A new beginning. In Christ, I was totally pure. I can't even describe the joy that I felt. My entire life was changed at that moment. My life had changed ownership. I no longer owned myself, and I no longer needed to make myself good. I was hidden with Christ, in God and I had been given Jesus' righteousness. My past was truly past, and I was a "new creation".[19]

---

[19] 2 Corinthians 5:17

26

I remember some of my previous attempts at being "good" and how much I had failed. I thought about the list of rules that I thought automatically came with choosing Christ. He began to show me that He had not been giving me a list of do's and don'ts like a prison ward, but like a good, amazing, loving Father. God knew actions would lead me off a cliff, and was calling out to me to walk on the narrow path that would lead to abundance of life, both here on earth and in eternity.

My perspective of God had changed. He was no longer a distant unmoved being that didn't care about my everyday life, but the highest source of love, mercy, and grace I knew. I felt His love like the love of a father. A really loving, holy, good Father that was willing to give His own Son so that I could have a relationship with Him. A dad that wanted to talk to me.

When God said, "Toyin, you are new. You are pure. You're forgiven. You're free. You're my daughter," that moment changed my entire life. I was branded.

My response was simple. I told God if He could love me as I was, with all my sins exposed, then He could have my life. Before that specific afternoon in my room, God was real to other people, but not to me. That was the first time I had taken the mask off to see who I really was and allow Him into that place—and there, I saw who He really was. In that moment of being seen, His love became real.

> *Until you understand the magnitude of what you have been set free from, you can't appreciate the depth of the love, and mercy God gives you in salvation.*

This single event is what triggered every other season and story of my obedience that you will read in this book. It is because of the love that He showed me that day and every day since. It was because of this fresh, joy filled experience that I committed myself to living my life like Caleb did in Joshua 14:8, following the Lord "wholeheartedly".

When I decided to do this, He made a statement to me that I have held onto since, "you will see what I can do with a life *fully surrendered* to Me". Learning to live a fully surrendered life was not easy. It took a very real breaking process to get me to a place of being willing to go anywhere God sends me, and do whatever He tells me to do.

I knew God was setting me up for a wonderful, thrilling journey of obedience, and I want to invite you into yours as well. Though this is something I still fight for today, I can truly say that I am a lot farther along in this journey than when I started. It is my hope that this book shows you how you can get to a place of wholehearted, abandoned, joyful obedience to His will. Here are three things to remember as you read.

Obedience is About Relationship

Rachel Gibson put it this way, "The obedience of faith only works when it's rooted in a person, not a rule. Imposed on its own, a rule invites us to sit in judgment, weighing its reasonableness. But a rule flowing from relationship smoothes the way for faithful obedience. When a child doesn't understand her mother's command, the mother's character plays a strong role in what happens next. A cruel, capricious mother is likely to meet resistance. But an affectionate, nurturing mother inspires trust, because you know she's on your side, profoundly.[20]"

Obedience works when it's rooted in relationship and not rules. Here's what I learned in those years when everything changed:

God is *not* distant or boring. He is not a prison guard, focused on having you follow His list of rules. God is a loving, passionate, exciting Father, Master, Leader and Savior—and He wants abundant life for you. He wants you transformed by His love. And walking in radical obedience to Him is the most exciting, freeing journey anyone could ever take. This is our eternal gift to Jesus. But it's much easier said than done.

Transparency

Many people ask me why I am so transparent about my life (both the wins as well as challenges). This encounter is one major reason. I never want to fall back into the trap of living a hypocritical life; living one way in public and having a different reality in private.

I would rather people see my weaknesses and God's strength and grace in me, than present a facade of perfection while rotting on the inside. I know how much God despises it. He set me free from it and I never want to return.

Healing From Abortion

Some of the women reading this may have had abortions. It

[20] Gilson, R. (2017, September 20). ChristianityToday.com

may be difficult to deal with the grief, guilt and shame that it brings. The same God who convicted me of the sin of my abortions, both healed and completely forgave me for what I had done. That is available to you too. So please don't ignore the abortions. Bring them to the God who is able to heal and forgive, and allow Him to bring comfort and mercy to you. You will be so much freer if you allow Him into that place in your heart. You will learn freedom in Christ. For assistance with this, please connect with a local Pregnancy Resource Center as many of them have post-abortive healing classes across North America.

Chapter 3

WHY WE DO NOT OBEY

Despite the amazing rewards of walking with a mighty God who has all the wisdom and ability to plan our lives, we often struggle to obey Him. Why is this?

As a Believer and neuroscience based Coach and Consultant, I've taught over 50,000 people, and studied the cross section between our intentions and actions, specifically the gaps between knowing what we want, yet watching ourselves do the opposite, or nothing. I've found there are two main factors that keep Christians from obedience: lies, and a lack of practical skills.

Lies

The enemy specializes in telling lies in his attempt to prevent us from receiving the fullness of what God has set aside for His children. He knows that if we are deceived into thinking that God does not care about us, or has abandoned us, there is no chance we will be willing or able to follow through when Abba calls us into challenging situations. Even on a foundational level, if we believe the lies of the enemy we can't hear the voice of God through the clutter.

Here are some specific lies that prevent many Christians from walking in the joy reserved for an obedient relationship with Christ.

"I'm Not Good Enough."

If you believe you are not worthy of God's love and forgiveness because of your past mistakes, or because you pray or worship differently from the "anointed" Christians around you. You won't believe God wants to use you in specific ways.

What This Produces:

This creates a feeling of inadequacy that deters you from even getting started because you feel like you wouldn't make the cut anyway.

What is the Truth:

The truth is that if God saw you as worthy of salvation (and He did the moment Jesus died on that cross on your behalf), then you are worthy to be used by Him. Ephesians 2:10 says, "For we are His workmanship, created in Christ Jesus for good works, which God prepared beforehand so that we would walk in them."

This is not a cliche verse but reality. There are specific works God has prepared for you to do and no one else would do it in the same way. His vision and plans cannot be hindered by your feelings of inadequacy. However, if you allow those feelings of inadequacy to stop you from taking action, then you give it the ability to hold back God's word over your life. Second Corinthians 3:5-6 says, "Not that we are adequate in ourselves so as to consider anything as having come from ourselves, but our adequacy is from God, who also made us adequate as servants of a new covenant." There is room for you in His story *if* you choose to break agreement with this lie that you – your ideas, your acts of obedience – don't matter.

"What I Do Isn't A Big Deal."

When you minimize the calling God has placed on your life, you allow the enemy to steal the level of impact God is wanting to have through you in that specific area. This looks like thinking, "I am only a _____". For example, a stay-at-home mom may think she cannot have a spectacular history with God because she feels isolated, doesn't interact with others often, and feels she isn't leading in a major capacity. This thought process often comes from comparing ourselves to others who we feel have a "more important" calling; people who are being recognized and whose work seems to be more widely honoured. This happens when we esteem what man esteems higher than what God esteems.

If you want to be set free from the spirit of comparison, you can start by learning how to see what God sees as more valuable than what people value. For example, when Abba would send me to places that had little or no honour – like preaching on the streets– I often had multiple people cautioning me and asking if God really sent me there. Afterall, there are so many other jobs I could be doing. However, I found that when God sent me to do other projects, like running for political office, I had a much smaller number of people checking to see whether I had really heard the voice of God. It isn't a bad thing. It simply demonstrates that even well meaning people have personal perspectives on what is "good" for you even though, that good thing may not be the God thing (at all, or for that season).

What This Produces:

Thinking that your actions don't matter produces Christians that are just going through the motions. You lose your vision for God-level impact and settle for doing the minimum.

If you have not learned to hear the voice of God, and even more to pursue His leadership with relentless dedication—no matter how large or little the task–it will be easy for people to distract and pull you aside. It will be easy to ignore the call of God on your life, and spend all your time focusing on other people's vision for you.

What is the Truth:

When the God sends you to accomplish a task, it becomes a big deal. Recently, a new coaching client shared that her goal was to take her business to $2,000 a month. She said it was a "tiny" goal, but it was a big deal to her. I knew she added that label because some of the other businesses my team coaches earn hundreds of thousands of dollars per month. I reminded her that there is no such thing as a "tiny" goal if it came from the Lord; pursue it wholeheartedly. And that's exactly what she did. And of course, she surpassed her goal by 114% despite it feeling like a stretch at the start, and has continued to grow her business from there.

God cares about your obedience in the small things. In fact, your obedience in the little things will often demonstrate your willingness and ability to obey Him in the larger areas. So your obedience in the smaller areas often matter more than what you would do on any platform.

Brother Yun, a Chinese house church leader and Christian missionary who was tortured and imprisoned for his faith said, *"We're not called to live by human reason. All that matters is obedience to God's Word and his leading in our lives. if God says go, we'll go. If he says stay, we'll stay. When we are in his will, we are in the safest place in the world."* [21]

"It's Too Late for Me."

As Christians, many of us disqualify ourselves from living a life of radical obedience because we've already tried and failed. We assume that God is no longer interested in us because we have let Him down. We mistakenly believe that we've strayed too far from God's plan, and it's too late to turn back. Often, we doubt God's

[21] Book: The Heavenly Man by Brother Yun

willingness to forgive us for our sins.

There's a misconception that being obedient to God means being perfect in every area of life. So when you make a mistake, you feel the discouragement but for some, it keeps them from taking steps toward obedience. This lie boils down to one focus — ourselves.

What This Produces:

Believing this leads to a sense of hopelessness and reluctance to obey. Afterall, why on earth would we try to step out in faith and do what God is saying to do, when all we can see is the myriad of ways we have failed in the past. It's easier to settle for the basic, boring, "wait until I die" type of Christianity.

What is the Truth?

The truth is your obedience to God was never about your power and ability to stick it out, but about His empowering and upholding grace which is available to you. You *will* fail. You *will* make mistakes. And when you do, it does not take anything away from God. It does not minimize the work of the cross where Jesus shed his blood for your sins. In fact, thinking your sin is too great for you to be used by Abba places your belief in your brokenness over God's gift of grace.

The writer of Hebrews compares the sacrifice that Jesus made on the cross with all other sacrifices. "For by one offering

WHY WE DO NOT OBEY

He has perfected for all time those who are sanctified."[22] He later continues in the same chapter, that we are to believe we are forgiven, accept that forgiveness and come before the Lord with boldness.

"Therefore, brothers and sisters, since we have *confidence* to enter the holy place by the blood of Jesus, by a new and living way which He inaugurated for us through the veil, that is, through His flesh, and since we have a great priest over the house of God, let's approach God with a *sincere heart in full assurance of faith, having our hearts sprinkled clean from an evil conscience and our bodies washed with pure water.* Let's hold firmly to the confession of our hope without wavering, for He who promised is faithful.[23]

Do you see that?! God literally tells us not only to feel free to approach Him but to come in *with confidence.* To allow our hearts to be sprinkled clean from an evil conscience and our bodies washed with pure water!

Stop allowing the devil to lie to you about the character of God. He isn't speaking here to unrepentant people, but to those who have a sincere heart before Him. He is bigger than your mistakes. And when He calls you to a task, He is able to complete that task in and through you. I love what A.W. Tozer once said—"You need not fear letting God down, for you were never in a position to uphold Him."

---

[22] Hebrews 10:11-14

[23] Hebrews 10:19-24

"I Can Do It Alone."

We live in a very individualistic society, where people are often told that any sign of dependence on others is a weakness. We rage against authority and any form of accountability. We say things like, "No one can tell me anything" or, "It's just me and God," so we try to overcome habits of disobedience by ourselves, without seeking guidance, support, or strength from God, or a community of faith.

What This Produces

Lone ranger Christianity produces a heart that strays from the faith. Why? Because as a human, it is in our nature to stray from what we know. When you are constantly being bombarded with temptation to take the easy road, cut corners, or be lulled to sleep by growing complacency, over the course of time, it is very easy to forget your passion and commitment.

What is the Truth?

Community is a tremendous gift. You need to be willing to place yourself in relationships that challenge you to greater levels of dedication to Jesus' will for your life.

When the Lord woke me up to pray (the season I spoke about in the Prelude of this book), it was like a match that ignited friends and family in my community. Many of them told me they had been sensing a call to deeper prayer but didn't quite start until I mentioned it. Then a group of us began praying daily together and have continued for months. What was more amazing, was that whenever it started to become a mundane routine, the Lord would share a word or a dream through someone else in our community, that would cause all of us to pursue Him with more intentionality.

Having accountability partners and being part of a supportive faith community pushes you in the journey of obedience. If you have true accountability and not just "yes" men and women around you, inaction will only last for so long. Eventually, one of them will say, "Enough talk, go and do it."

Once a client had mentioned to me that he was really struggling with his business. He felt that Jesus had told him to change his pricing and increase it to reflect the level of value he provided in the program. He was afraid to do so because he wasn't selling consistently at the lower price. It didn't make sense to increase it. When we spoke, I asked him "So, what do you expect me to say, ignore God's leadership in this situation?" Absolutely not. The other clients in my Millionaire Mastermind who were in the room lifted their hands as a joke as if to shrug. As his business coach, I vetted the content of his service, the value it provided his clients and I let him know the price change was worth it. He changed it to the price he received in prayer (which more accurately reflected the value). Within the next 2 weeks, he had had more clients come into his business at the higher price point than the previous months. We still have a running joke now and whenever he gets clients, we lift our hands and shrug as if to say, "I guess Jesus knows better than we do."

In Chapter 1, I spoke about King Saul obeying God 90% of the way. It's easy to judge him from afar, but at least he had someone in his life who could call him out even as a King in Israel. Unfortunately, many of us have made ourselves kings and queens and have adopted a heart posture that is not willing to receive correction. This means that when we go off track, it sometimes takes us months and even years to notice, and even longer to turn around. You need to submit yourself to relationships that will challenge you to greater levels of dedication to Jesus' will for your life.

"God Doesn't Talk to Me."

The final lie that hinders obedience is the belief that God doesn't speak to you, or doesn't care about the practical details of your life, only spiritual areas like prayer and worship.

What This Produces

This produces Christians who behave like slaves instead of children of God. We have two different lives: The part of us that we are willing to discuss with God, and get His leadership and direction on, and then we have other areas of our lives where we feel we need to figure things out on our own.

In my book, *Money Mindset SHIFT. Church Edition*, I share about how many Christians are afraid to bring their practical needs and wants before God. They figure He can take care of their spiritual needs like peace, joy, love or anything else they consider spiritual like deliverance and healing. Yet, when it comes to the temporal needs, they feel they are on their own. They figure they have to sort things out on their own and if things aren't working, well that's just God's will. When you think that God speaks to everyone else but you, you tune out the conversation and miss even the most obvious cues He sends you.

What is the Truth?

When you are free to hear God's word and leadership in every area of your life, your whole life becomes a platform for His glory to be displayed. You get to pursue those goals and dreams with Him! You will be able to tap into His wisdom which brings His supernatural activity into your planning and thinking process. You are His son/daughter. If you need something, ask Him. Do not feel like you have to hide behind His back to get your finances on track. If He doesn't want you to have that thing and you are open to hearing His voice, He will let you know! It is a conversation. This is a relationship.

A Lack Of Practical Skills

We can't blame the devil and his lies for our lack of obedience all the time. Sometimes if we haven't done the personal work of growing in self-mastery skills, it becomes extremely difficult to follow through on the things God calls us to. We simply don't have the mental stamina to handle the task ahead of us because we haven't done the work to create that muscle in our lives which can hinder our ability to obey Abba.

It is often habits like laziness, procrastination, fear and not our lack of ability that keeps us from experiencing the fullness of God's call on our lives. And while you can always pray to change these habits, there are practical things you also need to do to change them.

Obedience is a muscle. This is why you may have noticed that the people who often have a history with God –stories of where He led them, they took action and saw fruit– often have multiple stories to share. This is because you learn how to subdue your flesh in this area and begin to follow what He says. However, It doesn't get easier because God is always stretching you further as you begin to build the *habit of obedience.*

Just like some have a habit of exercise, there is a habit of following God's leadership. Just like exercise, where you continue being stretched, while it doesn't feel great all the time, eventually you feel the amazing effects of a healthy and strong body. And the more you do it, the better it gets. That happens when you're building a habit of obedience. You are continually stretched and He will often give you assignments that are greater than the last.

When you first start exercising, you don't start lifting 100lb weights, you work your way up to it. In the same way, God often starts with small acts of obedience and then grows that muscle until you are able to do what you currently think is impossible.

I will share some of those skills here, so that you have the foundational stamina to withstand the challenges that arise when you step into obedience. We will explore them in greater depth in the coming chapters.

Faith

Faith is the foundation of obedience. Trusting in God's wisdom and goodness is what will give you the motivation and confidence needed to obey His commands, even when they seem challenging or unclear. Most people think faith is something that you either have or you don't. But it is something you can develop over time. This is not referring to the faith needed for salvation, but the gift of faith and the ability to take God at His word and step out of the boat when He calls you. Faith is not automatic, it is a learned process. It is learned through time in the Word of God, time in prayer, and in action, through practice.

Courage

Obedience will demand that you walk in courage. Stepping out in obedience often requires you to leave your comfort zone and face unfamiliar territory. And the ability to intentionally leave what is familiar and comfortable, is once again, a learned skill. This is why in Joshua 1 when it was time for Joshua to take over leadership of the people of Israel and bring them to the promised land, God reminded him four times to "be strong and of good courage"[24]. You will need to have the courage to stand up for what the Lord has called you. You will need courage to follow His guidance despite external pressure, especially when you face adversity or opposition, because you will.

---

[24] Joshua 1:6,7,9,18

Self-awareness

People who are not self-aware have a difficult time trying to be obedient. Without self-awareness, you don't see your own weaknesses, or blind spots. So when Abba is wanting to direct you, you are more susceptible to distractions, self-sabotage, and making mistakes that could easily have been avoided if you were simply more honest with yourself about those areas of weakness. For example if you know that an area of weakness is procrastination, you are more likely to catch yourself in the middle of that instead of waking up 6 months later wondering why that project didn't go anywhere.

A lack of self-awareness also means that you may be unaware of your own strengths. So when God calls you to complete something well within your ability, you waste time and energy battling with feelings of incompetence rather than just getting it done. Like Moses, who was uniquely anointed to deliver the Israelites, but started the journey with much internal turmoil because he couldn't see the potential in himself. Or the people of Israel, who turned an 11-day journey into 40 years[25]. Their constant complaints and propensity to fear, caused God to declare that no one from that generation would step into the promised land. When you are aware of your patterns of self-sabotage, and the "foxes that spoil the vine"[26], you can set up accountability to avoid the traps the enemy sets on your path. This will help you to overcome and finish the work you have been given to do.

---

[25] Deuteronomy 1:31-36

[26] Song of Solomon 2:15

Discipline

The amazing advances in technology –while helping us accomplish more in shorter amounts of time– have often made things so easy that we have forgotten how to discipline ourselves. We don't need to leave our couches if we want to eat food. We can simply open one of many apps, order the food, and have it brought fully prepared to our door. We don't need to use the stairs, or elevator, and we don't need to stand over a stove or wait on a slow cooker.

Discipline means having the self-control and consistency to get things done. And I've learned that discipline in one area will lead to discipline in other areas. This is the reason our clients will often breakthrough in multiple areas of their lives when they come to us for one. For instance, they learn discipline in their finances, and in the next two months they also lose 30 pounds, or finish writing a book soon after. Discipline is contagious and is necessary to follow through on what God has called you to do.

Grit and Perseverance

I call this "bouncebackability" in my coaching programs. Obedience is a lifelong journey. You will need stamina to stay humble when things go well, and perseverance to endure when you experience setbacks. This is not automatic. Many people quit before they ever really get started. If you want to obey Abba, you cannot continue to quit so easily when things get difficult. Being able to "stick it out" is a learned skill. When new staff members start working with my company, they often say the first month is like drinking from a firehose; meaning they often get overwhelmed. Yet once they've built the muscle, years later they do the same tasks that would have caused overwhelm in year 1 without really having to think about it.

In fact, when God sent me into business, He knew that this was an area of growth for me and said, "You haven't done it until you've done it for 10 years minimum." Whew! He knew that there would be moments I would want to quit. This was especially true in the beginning when I was so bad at the business that we had no money. I would need His reminder to persevere through the difficulty. Even today as we have grown and multiplied, I still remind myself that we haven't yet begun until we've done this for 10 years. It's crazy to think that at the time of this writing, we are in year 8. We're recognized as the 74th fastest growing company in Canada according to the Globe and Mail's Top Growing Companies Of 2023 Ranking with a verified 592% growth over the last 3 years. God knew that our perseverance would be necessary to see fruit.

Humility

Obedience will teach you humility. You need this for longevity. When you think too highly of yourself, or take yourself too seriously, this makes failing or missing the mark 10x more painful than it would be. It takes the weight off when you accept that, left to your own devices, you have nothing to bring to the table, and everything comes from Him.

One of my favourite verses is Psalm 103:14: "Just as a father has compassion on his children, so the Lord has compassion on those who fear Him. For He Himself knows our form; He is mindful that we are nothing but dust." God knows your weaknesses more than you do, and still chose to call you. Stop complaining and step out into what He's said to do.

Knowledge of Scripture

You cannot obey God without knowing what He has to say about your actions. Many Christians want to have a lifestyle of obedience but are too busy to read the Bible. Listen, there are no shortcuts with Abba. There's no checking Cole's Notes to give a summarized answer. Knowing God's Word and character provides a clear foundation for making obedient choices—*especially* when the pressure is on and you have limited time to think about your response to a situation. Often, the scriptures I have memorized will come to the surface right when I ask the Lord for wisdom.

Your inability to obey may not be because you don't care to. It may come from these two roadblocks—believing the lies of the enemy, or not having built the muscle to follow through to the end. This was one of the reasons we created our Self Mastery Academy, to assist people in learning how to discipline their brains and bodies to finish what they start.

My Birth Experience - The Unexpected Obedience Crash Course

I've always read where the Bible says we are redeemed from the curse and I believed it, except the part about being redeemed from the pain of childbirth. To me, that was just how it worked. I had two of my mentors mention that they had "joyful" births, and a friend who barely noticed that she was in labour, and that always made me curious. How is that possible? Is that available to me? How could I access it? When I was pregnant with my third baby, I decided to actively bring the process of pregnancy and birth to God and press in to see this scripture fulfilled.

For context, my first birth process produced a healthy baby, healthy mommy, with no complications, but it was a horrible hospital process. To make a long story short, they ignored me, belittled me, and leveraged fear for every decision they wanted me to make. "We think you should ___ and if you don't, you're putting your baby's life at risk."

At the end it turned out I was right about my body, and everything I had been telling them. It was the mercy and grace of God she was okay and I was as well, because they ended up putting both of our lives at risk and admitting their fault. During that birth I was angry, sad, frustrated, and had so many negative emotions. I promised myself that it was non-negotiable for me to advocate for myself on the next birth.

For Baby number two, I went to the hospital aware,

prepared, and strong minded. No one was going to push me over. The primary emotion was "determination" and while it was a good experience overall, it was still a fight or flight reaction from the first birth. However, there was one moment that shifted things. As active labor started, I randomly looked at the clock–it said 3:30 pm– and I thought, "This baby will be out in an hour, and not a minute more." Imagine my shock when I looked up at the clock the moment my son was born, and it was 4:30 on the dot. I thought, "Whoa! That was available to me? What else could I have requested?"

Fast Forward

A year later I worked with a coach who taught me about being aware of my body in order to heal long term physical pain, my vocal chords etc. It was bigger than healing pain, it was learning to listen to what my body was telling me. I had pushed and grinded for over a decade; it was the first time I noticed my body needed care or I would not finish the work I've been sent to do because of wear and tear.

When I found out I was pregnant with my third baby, I decided to leverage what I had learned about engaging with God in the "non-spiritual" areas of life. I was no longer ignoring my body, and for the first time, dreamt big about birth. Instead of survival, fight, or flight I wanted those experiences I had heard about, and started praying, envisioning this amazing process, and being grateful in advance. It was going to be a dream!

Then the first 6 months of pregnancy slapped me sideways.

I got sick with the most random things. I had horrible morning sickness which kept me on my couch for 3 months. I recovered, then got covid. I recovered, then got food poisoning. I recovered from the food poisoning, but that led to other gut issues, which took 3 weeks to resolve. I recovered, then lost my voice completely for a month because of the lingering covid cough.

I'm usually healthy, and I didn't experience anything similar in my first two pregnancies; like WETINNNNN (Nigerian pidgin language for "WHAAATTTTT")? The resounding message through all of this was rest. I couldn't work like normal. I couldn't "muscle through" like the others. My friends and clients know that I don't like to waste minutes, much less weeks, or months, and in the beginning I resisted it.

Every time I tried to get back on the saddle, Abba patiently sat with me, inviting me to rest.

I had to rest, then rest, then rest until I finally surrendered and accepted the season. Here's what was funny about all this. In January of that year, Abba told me, and I had written multiple times in my journal that it would be my year of *rest* and manifestation. When it came to manifestation, there were so many dreams that came true that year. Prayers I had prayed for years came through that year. But when He said it would be a season of rest, I really thought He meant in September, after I had the baby. No, He meant a whole 10 months of the year.

I envisioned birth day like my personal super bowl. I

reconnected with my coach, and he reminded me to focus on this amazing opportunity to have a phenomenal birth. I created a care-plan for myself and committed to not trying to be the strong woman who bounces back 3 days postpartum into full time business mode, which is what I did last time. I committed to slow down and care for myself and the baby. This time, I also had a midwife who was with me throughout. It was so different from my hospital experiences.

I wanted a water home birth. When my dad heard, he shook his head but prayed a strong Nigerian prayer that all would be well. I wanted to feel calm, centered, confident, and joyful. I wanted to be fully aware of what was happening and connected with my baby girl. The day before labor I could feel that my body was transitioning. I told my family and staff team, the baby's coming in the next 24-48hrs, even though it was 1 week early. I was awake that night just excited about our baby arriving, talking to her in my belly. I texted my sisters, "Yayyy lower back pain! She's definitely coming soon!" At about 3 am, I could feel her move differently in my belly and I said out loud, "Baby girl, what are you doing," as a joke, and right then my water broke! I thought, "Okay girl, you know what you're doing!" It was like we were communicating!

My midwife's teammate told me, "You're having too much fun, get some sleep, it's about to be work!" I took a crash course with an amazing birth coach, Tamara Youngberg, during early labor and learned so much. She mentioned that if you can overcome the emotion of fear and maintain calm, you can actually release endorphins in your brain which would be a natural pain inhibitor. She gave so many tips for overcoming the fear, and practical steps to understand the process and remain calm. As a Neuroscience Coach, I geek out on the neuroscience of anything and love brain hacking. I knew that our brain is able to create positive emotion with intentionality so it immediately made sense to me.

In active labor, I requested worship music and the presence of God filled the atmosphere with peace and calm. So much that even though I could feel the pain and pressure, I was so completely still and calm with my head against Josh's hand, that my mum said, "Toyin now is not the time to fall asleep!" And I whispered, "Trust me, nothing in my body is asleep right now." But that was my goal, to be so calm in the midst of the pain and pressure, it could be mistaken for sleeping. Her question let me know this was really happening the way I had prayed for it.

When the baby was about to be born, I treated it like the Superbowl. I told the midwives when she was going to join us, and shouted, "Hallelujah!" when she did. The supporting midwife said, "This has to be one of my top births of all time. Who laughs and smiles before the final push?" It was glorious.

This made me realize how intentional God was about birth. He allows labor to be intensive, and pregnancy to sometimes be challenging, so that we could keep this joy set before us as something to push for. I was so full of joy, and laughter, I got a deeper understanding of those Bible verses about enduring pain for the joy to come. What was even greater, this season of childbirth taught me lessons that I could take into the coming seasons of seeking to obey God at greater levels.

Lesson 1. ACCEPTANCE.

I learned that the sooner you can accept your hand, the sooner you can enjoy the gifts it brings. I accepted that my season doesn't need to look like anyone else's. A lot of my dearest friends, mentors and colleagues had long passed their child bearing years, so having a child in 2019 and again in 2022, meant intentionally slowing down in business, and ministry. Mind you, "slowing down" for my company looked like 5x-ing our business while I was pregnant in 2019 year over year and 2.5x-ing in 2022.

At the beginning of that season, I created internal suffering around the fact that people were building on their momentum while I kept starting and stopping. I would think to myself, "People are literally running and building and here I am, with my head over a toilet bowl, throwing up lunch and dinner in one go. I can't even get off my couch or look at a laptop." But over time, instead of comparison and complaint, I learned to accept that phase of my life. I accepted that:

- I love children. I worked at a camp for years. I know countless camp songs and games, and am a "fun mum" when I'm not fighting to stay up because of pregnancy.
- I love *my* children. I love their ages even if my peers had teenagers who didn't need to be cared for at all times. I

love their high pitched voices, their hilarious thought processes, and the fact that they come to our bedroom to wake us up every day. Our son saying lellow for yellow, and basgetti for spaghetti and our daughter celebrating missing teeth. Even on the challenging days, I reflected on how tremendously grateful I was that God chose to entrust me with bringing life to this world.

- I accepted that I wanted this season. No more waiting for the next one. No more belittling my progress; just acceptance and gratitude. I left comparison behind and owned that maintaining a multimillion dollar business, leading a team, serving hundreds of clients each year, coaching a Mastermind program intimately, and watching them scale their businesses and careers in the midst of this wild season was ample reason to celebrate.

Lesson 2: OBEDIENCE TO JESUS CHRIST.

September of the previous year (2021), I had a life changing God encounter; He gave me specific instructions for my business that stretched me. I had not been running my business full time for 11 months because I was running politically. After being "out of the game" for this long, on my return He had me invest almost $100,000 into systems, additional training, agencies, and so on. The money I invested came from our reserve profit account, not from active cashflow or revenue.

We hired 7 people to fill roles needed to scale. Abba told me to record videos, ads, start a new marketing funnel, redo a ton of trainings for my clients that I had been talking about for months, along with other things. He gave me a deadline of December 2021. I had 4 months to do what could have taken me a full year.

It was scary, uncomfortable, and difficult. I felt the pressure right into Christmas, but I did all of it. What I didn't know at that time was that I would be pregnant, have morning sickness, and have to completely focus on my health for a majority of the next year once January hit. God knew. He knew and when that time came, I had assets, agencies, team members who had been trained and prepared to step in.

Obedience in one season will assist your obedience in the next. Like I said earlier, it's a muscle that builds on itself. When God says jump, jump at that time. Stop delaying and wondering why things don't feel "aligned". You will find alignment when you submit yourself to Abba's timeline.

Lesson 3. JESUS CHRIST IS THE ONLY UNCHANGING ANCHOR.

During that year (2022), there were so many unexpected turns that at different points I didn't even know what to believe for, or how to "hold on to my faith". What gave me hope through all of it was this: Jesus Christ is Lord of my life. And when I die, none of this will matter. I will not take my business to heaven. I will not take my marriage, being a mom, my bank accounts, investment properties, or streams of income with me to heaven. I will not take friendships, or opinions with me either. Nothing goes with you into eternity.

The only thing that matters is if I believed in Jesus Christ as the Son of God and accepted forgiveness for my sins through his death on the cross, then my name is written in His book of life, and my eternal future is secure in Him.

In the challenges, I knew we submitted to His will and direction as much as possible. We prayed about the major decisions we made. We trusted Him with the outcome of it all. We clung to Him when it felt like the ground was shifting underneath us, and every single time He brought us through even when it didn't look like what we wanted at first. In fact, this is why we named our sweet baby girl "Hope". Because Christ is our living hope and outside of Him we would crumble.

There are so many moments I just sat in His presence, in worship, and cast my cares on Him. And every time, He carried it on my behalf.

That August, when I couldn't speak or sing, I learned how much we take for granted, being able to bring Him the gift of worship from our lips. There were so many times I was genuinely scared. Having covid during pregnancy, I thought, "will we be okay?" Or, "It's been 3 weeks and I still can't say one word, this isn't getting better." Or asked, "God please preserve my voice; it's one of my greatest assets." I also wondered, "Who am I without my voice? Is my identity rooted in Him or my ability to sing and communicate?" All the time, He never judged me for my fears. Just loved me, gave me wisdom for each step, and filled my heart with peace beyond understanding.

I have tears in my eyes as I write this. He was so kind to us in that season. He knew I needed to learn these lessons but wouldn't allow the season to break us. Through it all we are more than conquerors and we don't have to fight. We get to rest, lean and trust, then take specific action in His wisdom. Note that rest is not ignoring the challenge. You need to take wise action; I still showed up, made decisions, and led my team through it all.

Lesson 4. GOD EXALTS THE HUMBLE AND HUMBLES THE PROUD.

I often pray and ask God to keep me humble, and that year, He humbled me. In fact, I believe that with the level of vision He was releasing through me in the years to come, the challenges of that year were a necessary experience to stay grounded. It felt as though He allowed things to be completely beyond my control, in multiple areas, to remind me that it is God that gives us the strength to be able to do what He asks us to do. Nothing comes from us. I know this, but that year, I learned it on a level I had not yet experienced. And I was grateful.

I make plans differently now.
I pray differently.
I lead differently.
But most of all, I lean (trust) differently.

I learned years long lessons when I decided to give my childbirth experience over to Jesus, and I'm so grateful for His leadership in my life. I am grateful for the precious gift Hope is to us, and all she brought along with her.

It also highlighted why accountability and community is necessary to pursue the Lord. In that year, I had to lean greatly on my support systems to complete the work that was before us. An entire village carried me through. People visited, prayed, believed with me, encouraged me, and held my hands up when I was too exhausted to hold them up myself. God is faithful. He is kind. He never fails.

When you decide to create a real history with God of consistent obedience, you have to start by getting gut level honest with yourself about why you have either slowed down in this area or haven't gotten started in the first place. There is work for you to do and timing matters. So take some time at this point, bring out your journal and pen and answer the questions below to see exactly what has tried to slow down your wholehearted devotion. Awareness is 90% of the victory, and being able to let go of those lies, and commit to building the practical skills I've outlined in this book, are the foundation for creating habits of obedience.

ACTIVATION POINTS

- Reflect on a time when you struggled to obey God's call in your life. What were the internal barriers that prevented you from taking action? Was it due to an internal lie, the lack of a practical skill or both?

- Take time to pray and ask God to reveal any areas of your life where you have been resistant to obedience. Are there any lies you may have believed about yourself or God that has hindered your obedience? Write them down. What does God have to say about them based on written scripture?

- Take some time to reflect on areas of your life where you struggle to follow through on tasks or commitments, especially those related to obedience to God. Identify any habits or patterns that may be hindering your ability to obey, such as laziness, procrastination, or fear.

- Consider how comparison has impacted your willingness to obey God. In what ways have you minimized your calling or felt inadequate compared to others?

- What are specific areas of mental and personal growth you can commit to in order to complete the tasks God gives to you with excellence?

PART

2

HOW TO OBEY

Chapter 4

BUILDING HABITS OF OBEDIENCE

After giving my life and heart to Jesus on my bedroom floor, I was committed to following Him in every way. But for the first few years, I struggled to obey. Not because I didn't want to follow. In fact, I would do what it was I felt God was asking me to do but with a lot of whining, complaining, uncertainty, and back and forth. After a few years of this, Abba decided it was time for me to learn how to put my big girl pants on. He began to teach me how to obey without constantly wrestling in the process. It all began in the season where I was deciding who I would get married to.

Learning Habits of Obedience

In my early twenties, I had a season of solitude I call my "cave season." I was preparing for the MCAT exam, but my parents' home was always busy and loud, with church members, guests, and friends visiting. So, I moved into my friend's apartment for three months to focus. While there, I paused communication with my friends, stopped attending conferences, concerts, or anything at all. When I wasn't studying or going to work, I used the time to pray, read the Bible, and get closer to God.

That year, I had been studying the life of Moses and was deeply inspired by His relationship with God. It is incredible to me the level of detail with which God spoke to him, and the quality and closeness of their conversations. Throughout the books of Leviticus and Numbers, almost every chapter has a specific reference to God speaking to Moses, giving him specific and clear directives and Moses' response in getting it done.[27]

To understand how much God valued His relationship with Moses, let's remember when Miriam (Moses' sister) tried to challenge Moses' leadership because she disagreed with a decision he made. God's response to Miriam was:

"If there were prophets among you, I, the Lord, would reveal myself in visions. I would speak to them in dreams. But not with my servant Moses. Of all my house, he is the one I trust. I speak to him face to face, clearly, and not in riddles! He sees the Lord as he is. So why were you not afraid to criticize my servant Moses?[28]

I wanted this level of closeness with the Lord and spent a lot of time praying for God to help me be as attentive to His voice and leadership as Moses was. I was blown away by the fact that when people attacked Moses; more times than not, his first response was to lay down before God and give it to Him rather than fight or try to defend himself. I wanted to be bold in the face of adversity, while maintaining humility like Moses did. I prayed, "Abba, I want that kind of

---

[27] See Number 2:34, Numbers 3:42, 51, Numbers 7:89-8:2

[28] Numbers 12:6-8 NLT

relationship with You. I want to be a friend like Moses was. I want to know You!"

Wonderful prayer, but when you ask God for a closer relationship with Him, He hears and will do what He needs to bring it to pass. He started to do this for me in a way I wasn't expecting.

After three months of seeking God in the "cave", I started to miss my friends and reached out to one of my best friends, Joshua, to catch up. Josh was like a brother to me; he played bass on a worship ministry team that I was the lead singer for. Often, while he drove me home from events, I would have my feet crossed on his car dashboard, asking for his "guy" perspective on why another friend of ours whom I believed I was meant to marry, didn't notice or like me. I would ask him, "Do I wear too much makeup? Am I not wearing enough makeup? Do I talk too much for him? Should I wait? Should I approach him?" Some friends hinted that *Joshua* and I should be something more, and I would shut those conversations down fast because I thought God had told me who I was to marry and I didn't want to deviate from that. Entertaining something else felt like a lack of faith.

Anyway, I asked Josh to visit me at my workplace. I wanted to catch up on what God had done over the 3 months. That morning when I woke up, my first thought was, "Josh would make a really good husband." Immediately I thought, "Where on earth is this coming from?" I started praying against the thought so fervently that the friend I was staying with ran over and asked, "Toyin, what's going on? Are you okay? What did you dream about?" I told her, "I had this thought that Joshua would make a good husband! But I know I'm supposed to marry someone else! This has to be a distraction from the enemy because I'm going to see him later today." We prayed together that I wouldn't be distracted by Josh and I would hold on to what God had said. Then I headed to work.

As we spoke at my workplace, he mentioned that he had been thinking a lot about family, and had a dream that he was in Walmart with his future son. Now, Josh is Caucasian and I am Nigerian-Canadian. When he mentioned his future son, I immediately thought, "I wonder if his son was mixed race in the dream."

GAH! "Give me a second," I said.

I walked into the washroom, looked in the mirror and said, "Toyin, what is going on with you? Joshua is your brother. Stop this." I returned and we kept talking. Later that evening, he started to say something, but then stopped part way as if he had spoken too fast and was trying to keep himself from saying something. I said, "What's going on? We don't keep things from each other." As the words came out of my mouth, I remembered what happened that morning. I knew that I definitely didn't want him to know about the thoughts I had, so I backtracked and said, "You know what? It's okay. You don't need to tell me." Josh knew me too well. He said, "That means there's something *you* don't want *me* to know." Lord, help.

He continued, "So, here's what we're going to do, I'm going to tell you what I was holding back, and you're going to tell me whatever you don't want me to know."

I thought, "this is *not* good."

Reluctantly, I agreed. I finished up my shift at work and after two hours of him beating around the bush, likely because he knew this was not what I wanted to hear, he took a deep breath and said, "I know you think you are meant to marry someone else, so I didn't want to bring this up. I don't want to confuse you, but Toyin, I love you."

"CRUD," I thought. Then he asked me, "What's going on with you?"

I told him, "Oh man, this is bad. I had a thought this morning that you would be a good husband. But here's the problem, Josh, you know I'm meant to marry somebody else. And you're going to marry someone else. The last thing we need is to be married to other people, and be thinking, 'what if,' or wanting to be with each other! We work together and this is going to confuse our work relationship. This is really not good."

So we sat in that apartment building lobby and prayed, "Abba, take these feelings away from us so that we can marry the people you've ordained for us, and not be distracted by this friendship." We knew we needed to address and end this distraction immediately. So we agreed to never bring the conversation back up again.

But, for some reason I couldn't let it go.

Previously, when other guys had suggested we should get married, I prayed and asked God, and it would be a clear no. This time, when I brought it to God, I waited for Him to say no, but there was nothing. Throughout the next day when I prayed, I heard nothing from God. Remember, I was in this cave season. I had been communing and conversing with the Lord about anything and everything for months, so it was really odd to me that He would have nothing to say about this. By that night, I begged, "God, please just say anything to me. Even if it isn't related to this question I am asking." Finally, I felt Him say, "I want you to double check why you believe this other guy is the person you should get married to." Yes! I figured God wanted to help me stay focused and nip this distraction in the bud.

I thought back to the first dream from years before that had me convinced this other guy was supposed to be my husband. In that dream, the guy was on a radio interview and was introducing his wife to the host. He said "My wife…" and then he paused, and I thought he was going to say, "Toyin." My dream-self responded, "No, don't let it be me," because at the time, I didn't like the guy. He proceeded to say somebody else's name. Somehow (don't judge me), when I woke up, I decided that the only reason he said someone else's name was because it was my dream and I was so against the idea.

So I brilliantly concluded that he was *trying* to say my name as his wife in the dream, but couldn't because it was my dream, and therefore he was the person I was supposed to marry! Yes y'all. This was a messed up, completely over-spiritualized process, but I believed it for 2 years. And of course, confirmation bias kicks in, and I had all sorts of clues after that point that strengthened that belief. Now, here I was 2 years and many tears of rejection later. When I thought about the dream objectively, I realized that this guy had said *someone else's name*.

"Whatttt?" I asked God, "Why didn't you tell me to review the dream 2 years ago?!" I had experienced so much heartbreak because of this belief. God showed me 3 reasons He didn't correct my trajectory earlier.

1. The heartbreak of those two years allowed me to feel again. Prior to giving my heart to Jesus, I had been in a destructive four-year relationship. Everyone around me saw how

it crushed me, but I never cried. Instead, I told myself, "I'm a strong woman, and no one's ever going to hurt me like that again." I became hardhearted. This new area of rejection had broken me down, which allowed me to bring all the pain from all those years to Jesus in tears. And while I cried from this situation, I cried about the rest and I was able to receive healing and closure for a lot. God said, "I wanted you healed these two years."

2. It kept me from getting distracted by relationships in a season of growth in Christ. I had about 3 different guys approach me over the 2 years about marriage. Because I thought I was meant to marry someone else, I could easily let them go and stay focused on my growth in Christ.

3. The guy had the personal awareness to simply share his disinterest despite how it made me feel. It was actually a great thing because it meant that my feelings never actually budded into a relationship, so I could stay focused on healing and growing in Christ.

Note how God uses things that may feel painful to protect and direct our path. I said, "Okay. If that's the case, why are you correcting me now? Is Joshua the person you have chosen for me?" I felt a tiny voice in my heart say, "Yes." But it couldn't be this simple. I needed more confirmation. Or did I?

Habits of Disobedience

You will either run towards Abba in the place of obedience, or push, wrestle and fight your way through. While many of us are familiar with identifying blatant disobedience, for example, the story of Jonah is a demonstration of knowingly going in the opposite direction from where God sent you. Most of us can think of an experience where God told you to do *this,* and instead, you did *that.* But there are more subtle ways we disobey God—and those are worth naming as we transition into active obedience.

Over-spiritualizing God's Call

One of the more hidden areas of disobedience is where God calls us to trust His voice. That was my mistake when I prayed about Josh. I heard that tiny "Yes," but didn't trust it. I was in a season of asking God to draw me closer to Him but when He did speak, I didn't want to receive it at face value. "I understand you want me to hear your still, small voice and follow. But God, don't start with a decision as important as who I marry!"

I called two friends and told them, "I think God wants me to marry Joshua, but I need confirmation. So I'm going to fast for seven days, and ask God if this is really what I'm supposed to do." One of these friends was someone who often looked for confirmation about his calling though it was obvious to all of us. In fact, I used to joke with him about it. I would say, "What are you waiting for? Are you looking for an angel to come down from a mountain with a letter, hand-signed by God, saying, 'You are hereby allowed to do this thing I have called you to do?'"

So now *he* says to me, "Toyin, are you waiting for an angel to come down from the mountain with a letter hand-signed by God, saying 'Joshua shall hereby be your husband'? Is that the confirmation you're looking for?"

As soon as he said that, I felt God speak to my heart directly, "You often ask for confirmation before you do what I tell you to do. In fact, you pride yourself in the confirmations you receive. But delayed obedience is disobedience. And you have created habits of disobedience. You've been asking to know Me, walk in My presence and be with Me like I was with Moses. But every time I tell you to do something, you wait for confirmation before you do it."

Abba reminded me of a recent event, when I was standing in line outside of a store. There was a woman across the road I felt He wanted me to share the gospel with. I ignored the inner nudge and stayed in line. I watched as she crossed the street and thought, "Wow! He's serious about having me speak to this woman; she just came to my side of the street." But I stayed put. She then walked over to our line and I continued to watch her silently. She walked up the line and ended by joining the group of people who were behind me. I was beyond excited. I shared the gospel with her and felt so excited that God would prove He wanted me to speak to her by bringing her all the way beside me in the line!

But when he brought this memory back to me, God showed me that this was another example where He has asked me to do something and I ignored that inner leading until I had the "confirmations".

There were so many other examples He showed of me waiting until there was a confirmation before taking action. Abba continued speaking, "Moses had habits of obedience. For the most part, he moved when I spoke. If you want a relationship with Me like he had, you need to be able to respond when I speak, like he did. You're learning to hear, trust my voice, and follow my instructions when you hear them. Are you willing to step forward in faith without having all the answers neatly provided?" It was hard to trust but I was ready to develop habits of obedience, where the wrestle and struggle was no longer a hallmark of my obedience to Him. "Ok Abba, if this is what you are saying, I'm in."

Too many of us over-spiritualize obedience. We tell God, "If you do not show me through this many confirmations, then I won't do it." Some of you, like the friend I spoke about earlier, are still waiting for "confirmation" to do the thing God called you to do five years ago. Yes, there are times where God wants to confirm His word to you. Like when Gideon asked God in Judges 6 to confirm that He was truly going to give him victory if he were to fight the Midianites. There are times when we can ask, "Abba, please make it a bit clearer." There's no hard and fast limit for asking for confirmations about what God is saying to you.

In fact, needing confirmation in itself is not a bad thing, especially when you are just learning to hear the voice of God. The challenge I was facing was that I had begun to learn to hear His voice but was still walking with hesitation and uncertainty. I was requiring these confirmations for everything God would say to do. Walking with the Lord is a partnership where over time, you learn to hear and move; to recognize the "cloud by day," or "fire by night,"[29] that step by step direction from God. And that comes from trusting His voice without needing to hear it from 5 different places. There comes a point where you need to take action; do what He said to do, when He says to do it, and stop waiting for the visiting prophet or a pastor's sermon in order to finally act.

Numbers 14:22 shares that the people of Israel asked for multiple signs but still didn't believe that God would follow

---

[29] Exodus 13:21

through on his word. He did not allow them to step into the promised land because of their lack of belief.

Don't worry about making mistakes. If you just start to do what you've heard, God will help you course correct, if you are wrong. He will speak into the situation, and He will show you where He wants you to be. But course-correction won't happen if you never start in the first place! How can a ship correct course if it never leaves the harbor?

Questioning God's Voice

Is questioning God's voice the same as over-spiritualization? Although they're similar, there are important differences. Over-spiritualizing is waiting for one or multiple signs of confirmation before making a decision. It's like saying, "Okay, God, I know you could do this. I just don't know for sure if you're asking *me* to do this. So, I'm going to set up all of these tests and confirmations before I do what you want me to do."

Questioning God's voice, on the other hand, means *not* trusting what He's saying, and then *not* following it. It's almost like looking at the scope of the challenge, looking around yourself and saying, "wait, are You talking to *me*? Are You asking *me* to do that?! I couldn't," and not acknowledging that God, who has called you into fellowship with His Son Jesus Christ our Lord, is faithful. He is faithful to strengthen you to complete whatever task He places in front of you. The example of Moses is instructive here. When God first called to Moses from the burning bush, He told Moses that he wanted him to lead the Hebrews out of Egypt. But Moses couldn't believe that God could use him. He gave God all sorts of excuses, "But God, who am I that I should go to Pharaoh and bring the children of Israel out of Egypt?"[30] "But God, no one will listen to me."[31] "But God, I stammer."[32] Finally, Moses just got really honest, "Lord, please send someone else."[33] Early in his walk with God, Moses questioned Him repeatedly.

But the book of Numbers shows Moses after he's been walking with God for a long time. In that book of the Bible, there is no argument between Moses and God. Numbers 17:11 says, "Moses did so; just as the Lord had commanded him, so he did." Moses simply obeys. Moses learned to accept God's word and obey Him the *first* time. And because of that, God was able to give Moses the first five books of the Bible. He gave Moses the specifics for the tabernacle. He gave Moses the laws for Israel. God expressed Himself to His people through Moses. He showed Israel His acts but showed Moses His ways.[34]

The Hebrew word used for "His ways" is "darak" and one of the definitions of this word is God's "path" or "manner". God showed Moses the "how" behind His dealings. The thought process behind His decisions. This is incredible! When God saw that Moses was no longer constantly questioning Him, He was able to entrust him with greater levels of understanding and responsibility.

As you walk with God, He will ask more and more of you. Sometimes He begins to entrust you with favor, influence, people

---

[30] Exodus 3:11

[31] Exodus 4:1, my paraphrase

[32] Exodus 4:10, my paraphrase

[33] Exodus 4:13

[34] Psalm 103:7

and/or money. The stakes get higher the closer you get to Him. That's part of why He waits and is purposeful about what He asks of you. If you really want your entire life to look the way He wants it to look—if you really want the fullness of what is available to you in obedience—you have to take responsibility for how you respond to His call.

Reluctant and Resistant Attitudes

We also disobey when we have a bad attitude behind our obedience. In my early days as a Christian, whenever God told me to do something, my first response was always, "No." Even though I had given Him access to my life, even though I *knew* I would eventually do it, I always had a period of dragging my feet and arguing with God before I would get to the Yes. Now that I'm a parent, I thought of this like asking a child to do a chore. They know they're going to eventually do it, but every time you ask them, they throw a tantrum first. When my own children do this, I think, "I know you're going to do what I've asked. Why do we have to go through this phase first?" But that's how I was in my attitude toward God.

At the beginning of my journey in obedience, I acted like a child. I had to learn maturity which looked like no longer choosing to complain before being obedient. And honestly, learning this was one of the major pivots that converted my journey in obedience from a grind to an adventure.

As I prayed to God about Joshua in that moment on the phone with my two friends, He showed me that every time He would tell me to do something, I would argue first.

God said, "Toyin, you want to have a relationship with me

like I did with Moses? Moses had *habits of obedience.* In the beginning, when I told Moses to follow me, he did the same. He said he couldn't do it. But he got to a point where he stopped the tantrums. He matured in obedience, and he started to do what I told him to do." Then, God reminded me of when Moses did disobey God. God told Moses to speak to a rock to bring water to the Israelites in the desert, but Moses struck the rock instead because he was so angry at their constant complaints. As a result, God did not let him go to the promised land. In Deuteronomy 1:37, Moses tells the Israelites, "The Lord was angry with me also on your account, saying, 'Not even you shall enter there.'" Moses did not see the promised land because he disobeyed God in that one thing.

God said to me, "Toyin, you don't want to be as close to me as Moses was if you aren't willing to change your habits. This is a shift you must make if you're going to walk with me as closely as you say you want to. You have to be learn to say yes without the resistance. To follow willingly. For your sake, I cannot bring you closer, because if you continue with habits of disobedience and you're as close to me as you are asking, you wouldn't steward that level of responsibility well."

It was a healthy dose of the fear of God. He was inviting me to see Him as He is. He isn't just a friend–He is the Lord of the Universe, the King of all ages–and to walk in relationship with Him and have His leadership was not going to be a flippant thing. He's asking the same of you. The more you see of God, the more His voice should cause you to respond willingly and readily. You can't say you want the excitement, adventure, fun, the relationship, and the rewards of walking with God, but not expect the Father to expect more of you. To whom much is given, much is required.

Consecrated but not Activated

Many of us are consecrated but not activated. We love Jesus, we are intentional in living for Him and doing our best to avoid sin, but, we are not yet activated in this place of following Jesus where He calls us outside of these basics. Obedience to Jesus is something you choose to do. However, just like many people don't enjoy physically working out, spiritual obedience doesn't come naturally to all of us. Instead, you build the desire by actively pursuing that thing.

> *"So then, my beloved, just as you have always obeyed, not as in my presence only, but now much more in my absence, work out your own salvation with fear and trembling." Philippians 2:12*
> *"But I strictly discipline my body and make it my slave, so that, after I have preached to others, I myself will not be disqualified."*
> *1 Corinthians 9:27*

Some of you may have had the desire for obedience but have held back thinking that lifestyle is only for "super Christians". For instance, you may think if you're not in ministry, on the mission field, or leading worship, then it's simply not available to you. But guess what? You can create the desire to obey God when you make the choice to do so. After you've developed and cultivated the desire, you then develop and cultivate the practice. Here's what that means: the more you obey God, the more you want to obey God.

Obedience is a Muscle You Can Train

If God had told me to do certain things at the beginning of my journey with Him, I would have fallen flat on my face or just run away. Over time, He has trained me for "larger" acts of obedience—but it's been a long journey, at a slow, steady incline. God works *with* you where you are today. Mind you, it might often feel as challenging as the first day because He will always call you to higher levels of obedience.

Think of this like working out. When you start building muscle with exercise or weights, you might do three reps. Then you work your way up to ten reps. The more reps you do, the more you can handle. The same is true when you're building spiritual muscles of obedience: you build and create a history of saying Yes to God, and you feel what it is like to be helped by Him as you go. Eventually, you can look back on your history and see the growth over the long term.

I remember when I was just starting to work out. One of the trainers at the gym told me to hang from the bar and do twelve leg ups. I couldn't even hang on for two leg ups! But a month and a half later, I was doing seventeen leg ups! I had conditioned my muscles. They'd been worked on and had grown. The same kind of progress is available in obedience if you simply demystify it. Remove all the stories about why you think habits of obedience are only for others. Give yourself permission to take ownership of your walk with the Lord. If you're not yet feeling the desire to obey God, start by praying for the desire. I still pray for that desire sometimes when I don't feel like it. I learned from Rees Howells[35] an intercessor in the 1900's to pray, "God, help me to be willing."

Rees Howells lived through World War I and God used him, his school of ministry, and group of prayer friends in amazing ways to impact the direction of the war. In the beginning of his journey, Howells was not willing to give up his life, but he sensed God might be asking him to do that. He ended up praying, "I am not willing—but I am willing *to be* willing." I love God because He welcomes even a weak Yes. It's still a Yes! God welcomes anybody who is willing to say to Him, "I want the desire to obey you. I know I don't feel it right now, but I'm asking you for the desire." He answers those prayers! But choosing the desire isn't the only step towards obeying God. You also need to know how to hear His voice in order to know how to move.

Ways to Begin

There's a catch in asking for this: you have to be willing to let go of your Plan Bs and really listen to what He has to say. When you hear Him, trust that He has answered you. Then, act based on the answer you've heard. Allow Him to course-correct as you move. Some of you have already done big things for Jesus and you know it. He's not telling you to start small. Your next exercise in building the muscles of obedience might be to stop complaining about your calling and to do your work with joy.

---

[35] Rees Howells: Intercessor, by Norman Grubb

At the same time, you may have never flexed this muscle at all. Your starting place might be to spend that extra time listening to what He has to say to you, right now. That might feel like a sacrifice, if you've never done it before, but He is pleased by that first step.

Maybe, you're afraid to ask because you are afraid of not hearing anything. Your starting place may be overcoming that hesitation and asking Him what He wants you to do! Or, maybe He's asked you to do something specific and you just need to begin. Whatever that thing is, start. Do it. And then, be consistent.

Consistency

An action only becomes a habit when you do it repeatedly. That means if you want to build muscles of obedience with God, consistency is key. I'm not as consistent in obedience as I want to be, but the truth is, I'm a lot more today than I was ten years ago. Why? Because I keep showing up. Here's what that goal means for me: each time God tells me to do something, I step into it. Every time. Even if I feel tired, I step into it. Even if I do end up complaining, I step into it. Even if I do it imperfectly, I step into it.

The beauty of consistency with God is that it brings so much joy. It's easy to get down on yourself when you feel like you've failed—and disappointment can easily cause you to break from consistent obedience. But the beauty of walking with Jesus *consistently* is in falling down and getting up again.

The Bible says a righteous man falls seven times and gets up an eighth time. It's about you getting back up, trying it again, and then repeating. That's what people do at the gym. Their body may be aching, but that's when the muscle is built; doing the work *after* you want to quit.

Prayer and Bible Reading

But how do you listen to God in the first place? A simple place to start is prayer and reading your Bible. It's not complicated. I already know what some of you are thinking because it's what I used to think too: "Boring." Why couldn't God speak to us through big airplanes writing His messages in the sky so it is extremely clear what He wants, or through sunsets, or some amazing mountain-top experience? He might, but He also sent us His Holy Word which has a lot to say about how we are to live if we look with a truly open heart.

Being with God means reading the Word and talking to Him. The Bible tells us what God has to say about everything we experience in life. Building muscles of obedience means seeking His face through the simple practice of prayer and Bible reading.

Then, doing what you hear Him say. It really is that simple.

If you failed to get into the Word yesterday—or the day before, or this morning—don't waste time beating yourself up. Instead, lift your face to His, accept His grace, and try again.

Accept Grace for Your Imperfection

Building habits of obedience doesn't require perfection. It

also doesn't require that you become some "super Christian." Give yourself permission to start where you are, and know that He walks with you through every small, quiet, "Yes." There are so many mistakes I've made trying to obey Jesus. I have put my foot in my mouth, often. Many times I've thought, "Crud. I wish I could take that back." I can't. In every single thing He's told me to do, I've fallen short. I *still* fall short to this day. But I know for a fact, He loves me anyway. I bring my mistakes, my shortcomings, my over speaking, and even my feeling of frustration to Him, and I receive His forgiveness and acceptance. I receive His peace, and then I keep on moving.

Whenever I make a mistake, God reminds me that I am still in need of His cross, His mercy, and His grace. To imagine that I had graduated from that with some sort of "perfection" would have been a lie and would belittle the cross of Christ. So, instead of shying away from my brokenness in the midst of my attempt at obedience, I acknowledged that I will never have it perfectly right and will need to lean heavily on His ability to follow His will. I remembered that His mercy is new every morning and allow that to stay with me. And I surround myself with people that I stay accountable to so that I don't preach to others and find myself disqualified.[36]

You're going to fail too, and that's okay. When you're anchored in love, He brings you into a space where He refreshes you and sends you back out. He heals you. If you're not anchored in love, you're going to quit when you fail. Remember His love and grace.

---

[36] 1 Corinthians 9:27

The Gifts of Salvation versus Obedience

Maybe it feels impossible for you to obey God immediately, whole-heartedly, and cheerfully. Wherever you're starting, God is willing to meet you there. He will speak to you, and He will lead you.

I want to clarify something: God's instruction on the path toward greater obedience should not be confused with the promise of His salvation. No matter how you might struggle to obey God, if you trust in His Son, Jesus Christ, you get the benefits of salvation. Even if your attitude is negative before it is positive about what He calls you to do. Even if you focus on the sacrifice, fear and all the reasons why you *shouldn't* obey Him, but eventually obey—you're still saved.

A friend, Derek Schneider, founder of the History Makers Academy, would often say that salvation is stepping into the doorway of a new house God bought for you. Consecration and obedience is what allows you to walk into different rooms and enjoy the additional benefits that come with that house.

A reluctant, fearful attitude about obeying God causes you to lose out. You're the one who ends up missing the joy of the process. You can either *enjoy* the process by giving Him your willing yes, or, you can suffer through the process and get the same outcome. Many people live their lives with an attitude of suffering toward everything. You could instead say yes, get over it, and step into the fun.

Yes to God & Yes to Josh

The night I agreed with God's still small voice leading me towards Joshua being my husband, all the confirmations I'd been looking for flooded in—from my mom, my sister, and my mentor—but only after I had said "Yes". While I was working an overnight shift, I prayed constantly. I knew that most of my people were asleep, but I couldn't wait to talk to them. I called my mom at 5 am in the morning. She picked up. "What's wrong?" she asked. "Is there an emergency?"

"Yes!" I said. "I think I know who I'm going to marry!" My mom was not surprised by my "emergency." She said, totally unfazed, "Is it Joshua?" I was dumbfounded. My mom says, "The Holy Spirit told me last September that he's the one you were going to marry." I couldn't believe it. I called my sister and she guessed it was Joshua as well, before I could tell her who it was.

Then, I called a mutual friend and mentor of his—still in the wee hours of the morning—expecting her to tell me something negative about him. She replied, "Oh yeah, I knew what was up with you guys. That's good. You and Josh are good."

Apparently, I was the last person to get the memo! The confirmations were gratifying, but, at that point, they weren't necessary. I had called them with confidence knowing that I had already stepped into agreement with that internal "yes."

The only person I needed to talk to now was Josh. My shift wrapped up around 8 am. I texted him and said, "After this shift, I'm coming over to your place. I want to talk to you." As I headed to Josh's house, I replayed our last conversation in my head-when we asked God to take away our feelings for each other, so that we could marry other people, and then agreed to never discuss it again. When I got to his apartment building, I asked if we could speak privately. We went down to the lobby—another lobby—and I cut right to the chase.

"I'm in," I said. "I'm two feet in. Let's get married."

I was not worried that he might've changed his mind. He had told me he loved me, and I knew it hadn't been a flippant thing for him. Josh asked, "Are you sure about this? You've been telling me for the last two years that you're supposed to marry that other guy." Yes. Yes, I had. I humbled myself and said, "Here's what the Lord has shown me over this past week." I began to share every realization, conversation, and prayer that had led me to this confident yes; yes to God, and yes to Josh. And that was that.

We had to bumble through the next part. We'd been friends for so long, it was a sudden shift to being in a courtship relationship. I'd always known Josh was cute, but we'd been friends for so long, I'd never cared a lick about being romantic with him. I thought it would be impossible for me to like him "in that way." But once we started courting, everything changed. We were praying for Jesus' help keeping our hands off each other! Even that—hilariously, and very wonderfully—was a confirmation.

Josh and I have been married over eight years. He's my best friend and the best partner I could imagine. Marrying him has definitely been my favorite act of obedience. In fact, I always say that second to the gift of salvation, Joshua has been God's greatest act of kindness to me.

He loves me so well that I often have to pray and remember that it's okay to be this loved and taken care of. God has used him multiple times to reframe my thought process on what unconditional love looks like and demonstrate to me my personal value in Christ.

This likely wouldn't have happened without God walking me through step by step, and teaching me about habits of obedience along the way.

God has so many gifts to give you—wisdom, love, adventure, abundance. Every time you say yes to Him, your habits of obedience get stronger, and your history with God gets longer. Like my friend Jenny Brown once shared with our Bible study, "Obedience is obeying God right away, all the way, and in a happy way!" Now, how can you fine tune your listening so you're confident you're truly hearing from God? That's what we're going to talk about in the next chapter.

ACTIVATION POINTS

- What have you heard from God, but are still waiting for different pieces of confirmation? Could He be calling you to trust His still small voice?
- Are you practicing habits of obedience or disobedience?
- What are some ways you tend to veer into disobedience? Is it in your attitude? Is it by resisting what you know He is saying? Is it by over-spiritualizing and waiting for multiple confirmations? Is it by questioning His voice?
- What was the last scary thing God asked of you? How did you respond? Did you do it? What attitude did you have if you did?
- How can you cultivate consistency in your personal walk of obedience with God?

Chapter 5

HEARING THE VOICE OF GOD

"It's time to step into full-time ministry." That's what I heard God saying, but how? I just had a baby, was about to finish maternity leave, and return to my part-time job. I usually worked five months out of the year to earn a bit to pay the bills, then we (Josh and I), would volunteer in full-time ministry for the next seven months. When I heard this, I thought He meant twelve months' of ministry work. No more job, and no more paycheck (as small as it was).

We were already struggling financially–which was fine when it was just Josh and myself–but now we had a baby. Josh was sensing a shift into entrepreneurship for himself and now, God was telling me to step into full-time ministry? "Abba," I said, "I've tried raising support and it hasn't really worked in the past. If you're calling me into full-time ministry now, how will we make it? I don't want to start and be unable to finish because of finances."

I attended a ministry conference and heard Wes Campbell, who read one hundred books about revival over the course of a year in Nigeria. He did this in preparation for ministry work and saw a mighty move of God following that. If I was stepping into full-time ministry, I wanted to see a move of God, so I decided to follow his example and read 50 books over the next 6 months.

One of the first books I picked up was titled *The Fully Funded Missionary.* Appropriate.

I didn't make it past Chapter One. The book asked a question that rocked me: "What are the beliefs you have about money that are based on tradition and people, not God and the Bible?" I realized that much of what I assumed about money had been shaped by my associations, not necessarily by Scripture. I put the book down and asked Holy Spirit to show me any beliefs I had about money that were not biblical, and the list was long. I then went through the Bible for the next three hours to test each of these beliefs (because I truly believed they were correct). I saw things in the Word I had never noticed before.

For example, He showed me the importance of financial planning. I always thought trusting in God to provide meant you didn't think about money at all. Instead, Luke 14:28-30 said "For which one of you, when he wants to build a tower, does not first sit down and calculate the cost to see if he has enough to complete it? Otherwise, when he has laid a foundation and is not able to finish, all who observe it begin to ridicule him, saying, 'This man began to build and was not able to finish.'"

I sought out mentors who had been full-time missionaries for years and other ministry leaders to learn how to be prepared financially. Those conversations showed me that many others were in the same place I was. Many were struggling financially, and some couldn't fully do their ministry work, because of the finances. I was so frustrated by this, that I decided to learn more about money, as well as share what I knew about becoming and living debt free. Mind you, while at that point I had learned how to live debt free, I didn't know how to build wealth.

This series of events culminated in Joshua and I starting a financial coaching business that has changed our lives, and many others. At this point, thousands of people have been liberated from financial stress—our clients have, combined, paid off millions of dollars' worth of debt. We've helped people increase their income by tens of millions of dollars. And, because of the success of our business, we have been able to support and participate in ministry work ourselves.

Listening to God took me from one stepping stone to another. He started off with an invitation to full-time ministry; then, prompted me to read a book that challenged my assumptions about money; then, He used my community to show me the need for financial coaching; then He showed me the one part of finance that I did understand very well and had already helped others to achieve- becoming debt free; then as I started the debt freedom coaching, He expanded my knowledge to see that I did not know how to build wealth or how to be comfortable with surplus because of my ministry background and showed me how to overcome that. As I followed Him step by step, it became clear that this "full-time ministry" calling was to the marketplace. By listening carefully, and coming directly to Him, He ended up giving me a process and system that has today transformed thousands of people's lives. I talk more about this in depth in my bestselling book, *Money Mindset SHIFT. Church Edition : The Top 9*

Myths That Keep Christians Stuck Financially and How To Get Unstuck, Live Debt Free and Build Wealth!

When God initially told me to go into full-time ministry, I didn't say yes for a few weeks because I couldn't see the full picture. Finally, as I sat in the pews at the Toronto House of Prayer wrestling with it, Joshua turned and said to me, "Toyin, if God sends us there, He's going to take care of us. Make a decision and move forward." I said yes, even when I didn't know how God was going to work it out.

Today, I run Bible studies, lead worship, speak, travel, and teach. I'm actually living out the life of ministry I'd always wanted, but it's different—and better— than what I imagined. All of this happened because I was willing to put aside my own ideas of what should happen next, and follow His directions—through His whisper, His Word, wise counsel, conversations with people, and through prayer. In order to do what God is telling you to do, you need to be able to hear what that is! When challenges come—and they will—the confidence that God is the One who sent you there will keep you going.

The Foundation For Hearing From God

Unfortunately, many people have made the concept of listening to God seem so complicated and out of reach, that folks don't even want to try. In this chapter, we're going to get into the practical side of how to hear from God. We will start with some foundational reminders: God still speaks, He can speak specifically, and He wants to speak to you.

God Still Speaks

Some argue that God spoke to people in the past, but doesn't speak today. Jesus is the same yesterday, today, and forever [37]. If He spoke directly to Moses, David, Solomon, Jeremiah, all the prophets, Mary, Joseph, and Paul—would He stop caring to direct us? Would He suddenly lose the ability to speak? He wants to, and is capable of speaking to us today.

God Cares to Direct Us Specifically

Throughout the Bible, we see God giving *specific* directions. He told Moses[38] how to set up the tabernacle, and gave Joshua[39] specific battle instructions about how to defeat Jericho. In the New Testament, God told Joseph[40] to marry Mary despite the unique circumstance around her pregnancy. God told him to flee to Egypt to protect the newborn Jesus, and when to return to Israel. After Jesus' ascension, God told Peter[41] to go to Cornelius' house, and there revealed His intent to share the Gospel with Gentiles. The Bible is full of instances where God weighs in on the details.

I remember asking God whether I should move out of my parents' house and live on my own. Josh and I were engaged, but we weren't planning to get married for two years. In Nigerian culture, a young woman doesn't usually move out of

[37] Hebrews 13:8 (ESV)

[38] Exodus 25–27; 30

[39] Joshua 6:1-27

[40] Matthew 1:20-25; 2:13-15; 19-22

[41] Acts 10

her parents' house if she's not moving into her husband's house. At that point, I'd been hosting ministry meetings in my parents' living room which would go late into the night. People would be singing loudly at 2 am and my family couldn't study, or get sleep. They never once complained, but I knew it had to be inconvenient as they led in other capacities. People visited at all hours of the day but I didn't feel free to increase the work we were doing, because it wasn't my space. I was torn. My parents did not want me to move out, so I prayed and asked God to make this really clear, so I would know it was Him.

During that time period, I opened my Bible to the next chapter in my regular reading: Acts 28. The last verse says, "[Paul] dwelt *two years in his own rented house,* and received all who came to him, *proclaiming the kingdom of God* and teaching about the Lord Jesus Christ *with all boldness and without hindrance.*"

Two years! His own rented house! To proclaim the Kingdom of God with boldness and without hindrance! This was exactly what we were doing with these ministry meetings! God gave me a specific, practical answer out of His word. He gave the clarity I needed to pray with confidence and fervency. Then He backed it up by miraculously providing the thousands of dollars I needed to move out, *and* touching my father's heart to give me his blessing to leave. You can ask God about the specifics of your life. He cares about the details!

God Wants to Speak to You

If you are going to clearly hear God's voice, you need to accept that He wants to speak to you. In fact, He might be trying to speak to you right now, in multiple different ways. But if you don't think He cares to, *you won't notice.* By just being aware that God *is* speaking and wants to direct your life, you will start to recognize His invitations. Bill Johnson, the Senior Leader of Bethel Church in Redding, California, once said, "God has no grandchildren." You don't need to be a "super Christian" to have God's leadership in your life. It's helpful to have people around you who can share their perspective, but you must take personal responsibility for learning to hear His voice.

4 Traps Inhibiting You from Hearing

1. Being Afraid of the Answer

People will often say to me, "I want to know what God is telling me to do in this situation. I've prayed for weeks, months, or years, and I'm stuck on this one thing." Most of the time, it's because we don't really want to hear what God has said. Often, we know what God wants, but it's outside of our comfort zone so we push against the very answer we're asking for.

God is not going to force His way on you. Look at how this played out in the life of the prophet, Balaam. In the book of Judges, Balaam asks God, "Should I go with King Balak and curse Israel?" God says no. Instead of accepting God's answer, Balaam says to King Balak's servant, "Well, you just wait right here. Let me go ask God again." He goes back to God with gifts and sacrifices, as if those things would change God's mind. God says no again.

Instead of accepting God's response, Balaam answered, "Even if Balak gave me all the silver and gold in his palace, I could not do anything great or small to go beyond the command of the Lord my God. Now spend the night here so that I can find out what else the Lord will tell me."[42]

God had already said "no" twice yet he told them to spend the night hoping that God would change His mind.

Finally, as he desired, God tells Balaam to go with King Balak. Difficulties plague him on his journey. Mainly, Balaam's donkey is not cooperating; it won't move forward and crushes Balaam's leg against a wall. Balaam beats the donkey and yells at it. God enables the donkey to speak to Balaam: "Why are you beating me? Don't you see the angel standing right in front of us with a sword? I can't walk through here."[43] Why did God speak through the donkey? Because Balaam wasn't willing to listen when God said no twice! Sometimes we don't want to accept what God has said because it's uncomfortable.

2. Circumstantial Faith

One of the biggest obstacles to doing what God says is comfortable circumstances. When we get very comfortable in our lives, we tend to want things to stay as is. After all, if God is making a way, shouldn't it be easy? But when you look through the Word, you find many areas where God calls people to do

---

[42,43] The story of Balaam and King Balak - Numbers 22

something, and it is far from easy.

In 1 Kings 22:13-28, the evil King Ahab sends for prophets to tell him whether or not he's going to be victorious in battle. Four hundred prophets tell him he will have victory, and only one said something different. That prophet, a young man named Micaiah, says "If you go to war, you will surely die," but he doesn't stop there, he adds, "and God has put a lying spirit on all the other prophets." Not surprisingly, Micaiah is thrown into prison, but his words end up being true: Ahab loses the battle. It took a lot of courage to give that word, when all the other prophets were saying the opposite. Though uncomfortable, he was hearing the truth from God.

The other extreme also holds people back. At times we'll say, "If it's too good, it must not be God," believing we have to suffer. Many believers step away from the very thing God called them to do when they start having the grace to get it done because we are not comfortable receiving God's rewards or blessings; we assume that God is only interested in our struggle.

3. The Spiritual Life

The third inhibition is one I shared already: over-spiritualizing God's still, small voice. This is the tendency to wait for that angel to come down from the mountain with a hand-signed note from heaven. In other words, we're waiting for some further miracle or confirmation. Remember, He will course-correct if we are moving toward Him in action and faith.

4. Motive

We hear what God wants, but our own self-oriented motives confuse us. I remember being stuck on a decision for a few weeks. I thought, "This is abnormal. What's going on Abba?" Then I slowed down to think about what would hold me back from receiving direction in that matter. I realized the answer was fear. I was afraid that with a specific option, I would be vulnerable to hurt. My self-preserving motives clouded my ability to hear God's answer. As soon as I was honest with myself, everything changed. I refused to be limited by fear. I thought, "Okay, cool. What if this person does let me down? What if I do get hurt? What's the truth?" The dialogue with God opened back up.

It's easy to say, "I want to live a life fully surrendered to God," or, "I want to love others more than I love myself." Until we can be honest about the areas where our flesh fights against our obedience, we can never step into freedom in obedience. The truth is, God's got my back. He's got your back. If He's telling us to be vulnerable, then He has a purpose. When we can give our tendency for self-preservation over to the Lord, we can hear His heart, however He chooses to speak.

Different Ways God Speaks

A common mistake we make is expecting God to always speak in a way you are used to. God will speak to you on His terms, not yours.

In 1 Kings 18-19, the prophet Elijah demonstrates to Israel that God is superior to the false god, Baal. He had a sacrifice and altar doused with water, prayed for God to consume the sacrifice, and God sent fire from heaven. He defeated and killed the prophets of Baal. He's on a high.

When Queen Jezebel heard, she vowed to kill Elijah. He became overwhelmed by fear and fled to the mountains. That's when God steps in to have a conversation.

God could have spoken to Elijah out of the wind or out of the earthquake or the fire. Given that Elijah had just experienced God raining down fire from heaven, that might have been what he was expecting. But in that moment, God came to him differently; He came as a still, small voice.

> **God will speak to you on His terms, not yours.**

The Sieve Test

When people ask me how I know which voice is God's and which is mine, or the devil's influence, I tell them about my "sieve" test. This helps me to sort out whether a thought, dream, circumstance, advice from a friend, etc., is truly from God. Like a sieve, I use this process to catch the good and release the bad.

Character of God

I first ask: "Is this in line with the character of God as displayed in the Bible? Does it help me to love Him with all my heart, soul, mind, and strength? Is it going to help me love my neighbor as myself? Or is it prompting me to do something sinful, like cut corners, or lie?" If it's telling me to sin, it ain't

Jesus. If it's defined by love – even if it's tough love – it may be from the Lord.

The Motive Check

Motives can be complicated. I often start with the simple question, "Am I motivated by fear, or by faith?" Why would I choose to do this, or not? God never motivates out of fear. On the other hand, God might be asking you to do something scary, but He'll motivate you, through faith, to get it done.

There have been so many times I've stepped out in obedience to God when my hands were literally shaking. I was sweating, my eyes were twitching, my heart was pounding, because God calls us to do scary things! But I knew He had sent me, and He gave me faith to continue.

"Does that Sound Like the Voice of a Loving Father?"

One final, and very important test to evaluate if you're hearing from God is: Does it sound like it's coming from a loving Father?

I remember asking a client of mine, "What is God telling you to do in this situation?" She responded, "I just need to get it together. I need to work harder. I never get it right." I paused, looked at her, then asked, "Does that sound like the voice of a loving Father?" She looked shocked and wept. She responded, "Toyin, I've prayed and all my life, the words I received were, "You never get it right." She continued, "Can you imagine? I leave prayer discouraged. Because of this, I never want to pray. Then I feel worse when I do pray, because I hear this voice telling me, "You don't even pray." This is the first time that I am examining the thought, and asking the question, "Does this sound like the voice of a loving Father?" I explained to her that even if she is doing something wrong, a loving Father corrects, but there is love and hope, even with the hardest corrections.

Finally, if the directive from God passes these tests, then I weigh any counsel received on the matter, and simply make a decision! Let's say you've been praying over something, and both paths align with the two questions above. In that case, choose one. Guess what will happen as soon as you make a choice? You will either feel peace about that choice, or the other choice will fight back, and make it clear that you should go with that. You know neither is sinful, but making the choice is what moves you forward.

Once the decision is made, move forward. Don't start thinking about all the other possibilities and asking, "What if... ?" Trust that God will course-correct when needed, so long as you continue to seek Him. Put your whole heart into obeying God's call.Let's discuss some ways God may be speaking to you right now.

1. The Bible

Hearing God's voice through the Bible is most important, because it guides our discernment for all other paths of communication. God's Word is the foundational place where we can hear and trust His voice. It is where we understand God's character and heart.

> *"All Scripture is inspired by God and profitable for teaching, for reproof, for correction, for training in righteousness; so that the man of God may be adequate, equipped for every good work."*
> *2 Timothy 3:16-17*

When you build the practice of reading the Bible to hear from God, He will use Scripture to highlight things that were not even on your radar. There are certain lessons that you need to learn that you may not be thinking about; when you read the Bible, God can bring them to your attention.

Secondly, the Bible teaches us *who God is*. That's the only way for the sieve test to be effective: knowing that God is just, holy, loving, merciful, and more. The Bible also teaches us how God expects us to live and what integrity looks like. We see that His will for us is our sanctification. He uses every experience in our lives to help us grow in holiness. It speaks very specifically to many practical, financial, and relational challenges we may face. And even when we experience situations where the Bible doesn't give exact advice, there are always overarching principles we can follow.

For instance, the Bible doesn't give advice about how often to log into, or whether to have social media accounts. What it *does* show us, is Philippians 4:8, "Finally, brothers and sisters, whatever is true, whatever is noble, whatever is right, whatever is pure, whatever is lovely, whatever is admirable—if anything is excellent or praiseworthy—think about such things." That informs what we absorb in our social media, entertainment, and even our news intake.

When you come face-to-face with challenging situations, and need to make split-second decisions, having Scripture hidden in your heart guides you. If someone hurts you, knowing the Sermon on the Mount will help you to not retaliate.[44]

This is one of the reasons I love the Word of God! I want to understand how God calls me to think, how to form my character and to make decisions. I want to know how He operates and what He values.

When we read the Bible out of obligation or as a checklist, it's boring and we miss what God is saying. For example, I would recite Psalm 91 growing up to kick off each new month with my family. But it wasn't until I re-read it after realizing that God wanted to speak with me, that the first verse leapt off the page. It says, "He that dwells in the secret place of the Most High will abide under the shadow of the Almighty." As I stared at those words, God spoke to me and said, "If you would meet with Me in this place of prayer and communion, you receive my guidance and protection." I remember thinking, "Whoa. How could I have been saying this for years but never really met with God in the secret place of communion?" Here was an invitation to draw closer to Him all those years and I didn't see it. The moment my ears were opened to listen for His voice, it made me want to *live* in that secret place.

So listen deeper. Before you begin reading, say, "Abba, what do you want to say to me today?" If you approach the

---

[44] Matthew 5-7

Bible with that expectation—that God loves you, that this is His voice, that He wants to speak to you directly—you're going to begin to make brand new discoveries in the most familiar verses. When you're in the Bible regularly, you stand on a foundation that tells you clearly who God is, and who you are called to be.

2. The Whisper (Our Thoughts)

The second way God speaks to us is through His voice. I don't just mean the audible voice of God. Some people *have* heard an audible voice of God, but more often, we hear Him through His whisper. A thought that comes up in my mind that does not seem to come from me; It often feels like something from left field. For example, at times when I'm journaling, I'll ask God a question. I have no idea what the answer should be, but as soon as I've written the question down, there's a response. I know in those moments that the answer didn't come from me.

Here's the thing about the Whisper: you can either believe He's leading you, or not. We tend to doubt God's voice through the Whisper, because we convince ourselves it came from us, and when we do that, it is easy to ignore. But the Bible says that He has put His spirit within us,[45] so it makes sense that He would communicate with us from *within*. Now, it's true that not every thought comes from God. That's why it's so important to apply the "Sieve Test".

---

[45] Ezekiel 36:26-28; Jeremiah 31:33; 2 Corinthians 1:22; Hebrews 8:10, and lots more!

3. Through The Supernatural

What we call supernatural is completely natural to God. He created matter and can do anything He wants with it. Throughout the Bible, there are stories of God acting in supernatural ways:

- God spoke to Moses through a burning bush that wasn't consumed.[46]
- He made a donkey speak to the prophet Balaam.[47]
- He confirmed His word to Gideon through dew and fleece.[48]
- He spoke to Saul through a blinding light, audibly from heaven, on the road to Damascus.[49]

And there are so many more. Supernatural manifestations are things that cannot be explained apart from God—things outside of our control. These supernatural events often come with a message. It can be tempting to write them off as a coincidence, because they are outside our realm of "normal." But when we do, we risk missing what God is trying to say!

A few years back, a friend of mine –not a Christian– reached out to me. He explained that he was going through an extremely hard time. He randomly thought that if he ever needed prayer, it was now. He said, "I thought of you, because you're the only person I know who does that, and I know you believe in God. Anyway, as I was thinking about you, and this prayer thing while

---

[46] Exodus 3

[47] Numbers 22:21-39

[48] Judges 6:33-40

[49] Acts 9

driving, and about how much I needed help, all of a sudden, as I drove, something fell on my car. It wasn't dangerous—it was just a loud noise at the top of my car, you know? But here's the weird thing, I wasn't driving past an overhang, there were no trees in the area, and there was no wind blowing. But there was this noise on the roof of my car."

Then He said, "I just felt like maybe God was knocking on my door, saying, 'I hear you.' How weird is that? So I'm reaching out to ask if you could pray for me?" For my friend, this was a supernatural manifestation. God was letting him know that, even if they didn't have a relationship yet, He heard him.

4. Dreams and Visions

Just like the Bible is full of supernatural manifestations, it's also full of examples where God spoke to His people through dreams and visions:

- Joseph has dreams of his brothers bowing down to him, which come true about twenty years after he'd originally had the dreams.[50]

- Solomon has a dream when God appears to him and says, "Ask me for whatever you want me to give to you." Solomon asks for wisdom and God answers his prayer.[51]

- God tells Peter in a dream that He has made all animals clean to eat. He says, "Do not call anything impure that God has made clean." Right after that, Peter is invited to preach the gospel at a Gentile's house—the kind of person

---

[50] Genesis 37 and 42:8

[51] 1 Kings 3

that Jews would have formerly avoided, because they were "unclean". Because of Peter's dream, he knows that the gospel is for everyone, not just Jews.[52]

- Paul dreams of a person begging him to come to Macedonia and share the gospel. After he directs his missionary journey to Macedonia, he and Barnabas end up starting the Philippian church, one of the most devoted of the early churches.[53]

Even the birth of Christ would not have had a happy ending without God appearing to Joseph in a dream. After finding out that Mary is pregnant, Joseph planned to divorce her and, "'An angel of the Lord appeared to him in a dream, saying, "Joseph, son of David, do not be afraid to take Mary as your wife; for the Child who has been conceived in her is of the Holy Spirit. She will give birth to a Son; and you shall name Him Jesus, for He will save His people from their sins."'[54]Joseph trusted God's direction through that dream, took Mary as his wife, and protected her. After Jesus was born, Joseph received another dream warning him that their family was in danger. As a result, they fled to Egypt and Jesus escaped the deadly plan of King Herod.

Recently, God spoke to me personally in this way! I was rolling out a new program in my company and I needed a name for it. My staff and I had considered names for weeks,

---

[52] Acts 10

[53] Acts 16:9

[54] Matthew 1:19-21

but none of them resonated. One weekend, I attended a ministry conference. This quirky guy came out of nowhere and announced he was going to pray for me. He prayed generally, and when he started to leave, I said to him, "Hold up. If you're going to pray for me, the thing I need most right now is a name for my new program, So please pray that God would give me a name!"

As he closes his eyes to pray for me, he laughs. He then said, "Actually, I'm not even going to pray for you on this one, because guess what? He's going to give you a name in a dream *tonight.*"

I didn't really believe it. This guy had no idea how long I'd been stuck on the name, and was now putting a time limit on when God would give me this name. That night at the same conference, there was a woman from Korea preaching. She was incredibly passionate. At times she was even yelling. At the end of her sermon, she invited everyone to pray out loud, and the room erupted into noise. In spite of how loud the room was, I suddenly started to yawn, I felt too tired to stand up and my head started drooping. Then all of a sudden—I woke up. That meant I fell asleep! I couldn't believe I had fallen asleep in the middle of an on fire prayer meeting. Was I snoring?

But then it hit me: I had a dream. And the *only* thing in the dream was the name of my program, The Master Key. This name fit 100% with our program, which is centered on hearing God's leadership and understanding His purpose for your life. He is our Master Key! The entire dream had been exactly three words. I was in awe that God had indeed spoken to me in a dream exactly like that man had said. He is ready to speak to you too!

> *"And it shall be in the last days,' God says, 'That I will pour out my Spirit on all mankind. And your sons and daughters will prophesy, and your young men will see visions, and your old men will dream dreams.'"*
> *Acts 2:17*

5. People

God speaks to us through wise and godly people. This is why community is so important. He also speaks through people we may not expect, like your child. Don't discount wise counsel because it comes from someone you don't agree with or in a package that doesn't look like you expected. It takes humility to understand that you can learn from anyone, and that God can speak through anyone.

Like I mentioned earlier, more than anyone else in the Old Testament, Moses was someone who regularly heard directly from God. Despite such a close relationship, God didn't tell him everything directly. Moses had a blind spot, and his father-in-law Jethro, was the one who helped him to see it. Moses was spending all his time resolving disputes among the Israelites and Jethro told him, "My son, if you keep doing things the way you're doing it, you're going to burn out."[55] Jethro gives Moses advice about how to delegate the responsibility of resolving disputes. Once Moses implemented his advice, it enabled him to lead the

---

[55] Exodus 18:17-18, my paraphrase

nation with better focus and greater capacity.

Moses was leading millions of people at the time and could have been too proud to hear what his father-in-law had to say, Jethro felt comfortable identifying the gap in Moses' process and was able to help him likely because he was approachable. Our dependence on one another keeps us humble. We do not have all the answers. We need people—mentors, coaches, leaders, peers, those we lead, and unexpected voices of reason—to call us out. You need people in your life that you can be fully accountable to.

> *"Where there is no counsel, the people fall; but in the*
> *multitude of counselors there is safety."*
> **Proverbs 11:14, NKJV**

Caveat

Don't allow people's critical advice to steal God's dream for your life. The people around you may provide wise counsel but don't prioritize people's voices *over* God's.

When I started doing consistent street evangelism, someone I respected dearly told me, "Toyin, you are trying to steal people from their home churches through your summer ministry. You're trying to start your own church." I knew she misunderstood my intent. I wasn't trying to be a pastor or start my own church. I tried to explain that the work was missionary type work, evangelizing on the streets and discipling new believers to do the great commission. She responded, "No Toyin, I see right through you. You're trying to start your own church. You need to back off, and not try to steal people from their own churches to join yours."

I was so stunned by her words that I started to seriously doubt my reasons for doing the street ministry. Was I trying to "steal people," like she said? I almost cancelled the whole thing. She had good intentions, but her opinion threatened to steal *me* away from the direction that God had given me. I asked another mentor about this to see if I was genuinely missing it. She asked me a lot of questions and then summarized what I had set out to do: "You want to train people on how to share the gospel. They are still attending their churches as they were before they met you. You're going to be finished your program at the end of the summer. Then you're going to send the people who worked with you back to their churches, to bring their learned maturity in service to their pastors and brothers and sisters. Did I get this right??"

I said, "Yes." She said, "Woman. Go preach the Gospel."

She taught me a lesson that day: I needed to use the "sieve test" even with advice from people I respected. When people give you counsel, be open to hear and receive it. Then, make sure it aligns with the Word of God, bring it to God in prayer, and run it past others to see if it really is from God. We never did start a church, or ever try to compete with other churches. In fact, by the end of the 3 years, new believers had been added to local churches. Pastors sent us videos and letters of gratitude for the work we had done strengthening their members in our discipleship program. Their members who had participated were now contributing to the work of God locally.

6. Wise Counsel

Wise counsel might seem similar to wisdom God delivers to us through people, but there's a difference. When I hear from God through people, it's random. I am listening to learn from anyone He sends to speak to me. When I seek out wise counsel, it's very specific, and it's something I usually initiate. This category includes hearing from God through your pastor's sermon, through worship music, going to a ministry conference, reaching out to a trusted mentor, or reading a book that inspires you to live more fully for God.

> *"Where there is no guidance the people fall, but in an abundance of counselors there is victory."*
> ***Proverbs 11:14***

When I know I'm being tempted to respond to some circumstance out of my flesh –like feeling angry about a situation– I ask my husband, or one of my best friends about it. I'll say, "I need to hear what the Word has to say right now. In other words, I don't want your opinion. And I don't want you to feel with me. I need the Word." I don't give all the details, but I share what's happening overall. Then I say, "This is how I feel. Please share some truth with me." These trusted people speak the Word of God back to my soul when I need it to come from the outside. Sometimes it's a corrective word. Sometimes, they quote scripture telling me I need to forgive: "Toyin, the Bible says we forgive seventy times seven." Or they might say, "The Bible says rejoice in all things. God's got this and God's got you."

When there are difficult decisions to make about the business, I will ask certain mentors to weigh in. Because of their experience, they often have a completely different view that I have no reference for.

I find wise counsel in many places. I find it in sermons, ministry conferences, worship songs; those are just a few on my list. His Wise Counsel can come through many different forms, so long as the source is consistent with His heart.

7. His Peace

Many of us pray for peace often. However, when we do, we usually mean a feeling of tranquility and calm. People say, "If I don't feel peace about something, I just won't do it." But Colossians 3:15 says, "Let the peace of God *rule* in your hearts." The word "rule" doesn't simply mean "to exist" it means to make decisions from a place of peace even if it doesn't feel peaceful. Peace is not a passive occurrence.

The peace of God doesn't mean you don't feel fear. God might call you to do something that scares you. I rarely "feel" a peace about things God tells me to do for Him. I am often shaking in my boots, but there is a calm underneath knowing it is exactly what God called me to do. Because of that, my surface feelings don't rob me of the confidence I need to still obey God.

Imagine David standing in front of Goliath, adrenaline rushing through his body. He didn't "feel" a tranquility about facing Goliath, but he had a peace and confidence in the God who was leading him. That's what letting God's peace rule over you is about, not just a calm feeling about what you need to do.

You take hold of God's peace by seeking it out in an active way. When you know you are operating under His leadership, God's peace can rule and reign in your heart.

8. Circumstances

God also speaks through circumstances. For example, in the story of Jonah, God told Jonah to go to Nineveh and preach repentance to his enemies. When Jonah tried to run away, Jonah ignored all God's subtle signs to turn around. So, God stepped into his circumstance. First, Jonah endured a storm on the sea. Then, he was thrown out of his boat and swallowed by a large fish. After three days in the belly of the fish, he was ready to go where God was leading. The fish vomited Jonah onto land, and he continued on to Nineveh where he preached God's message and witnessed an entire city repent for their wickedness.

Here's the caveat for circumstances: they are often used as an excuse for disobedience. There is a very strong difference between God taking something off the table, versus allowing you to encounter something difficult and expecting you to press through in order to break through. God will lead us through many challenges; but that's exactly where He wants us.

For instance, during our time in Kansas City, we experienced such crushing poverty. We went through one of the hardest seasons of our lives as a family. But we knew without a shadow of a doubt, God wanted us there. Suddenly, our circumstances changed. We found out they had filed our visas incorrectly at the border; we had to leave Kansas City and return to Canada. We didn't leave because it was hard. We left because we wanted to honour their government. God used the challenging time in Kansas City to teach us new lessons about our finances. God also used the timing of the return to Canada to provide for us and make sure we would be taken care of after the miscarriage that took place soon after. He can work and teach us through any circumstance, so long as we are looking to Him for wisdom through all of it.

9. Random Gestures of His Love

Sometimes God will communicate to us through the most random things, like butternut squash soup. During my first pregnancy, I wanted soup. Like, I *really* wanted soup. My husband took me to the local Tim Horton's (a Canadian coffee shop). They usually had soup on their menus, but they didn't have soup at this store. He took me to another Tim Horton's. They didn't have soup either. He took me to *four* Timmy's. No soup. I was getting agitated. Josh took me to two Subway restaurants. Still, no soup.

After six stores we gave up and went home. I was hangry (hungry and angry). "Why do they have soup on the menu if they're not going to have soup in the store?" I griped. I started looking at pictures of soup, and reading soup recipes online while complaining. God said to me, "Is soup worth getting offended over? You can say you're pregnant and you're having cravings, but now you're using it as a license to complain and sin." I repented for my sour attitude, surrendered this random desire for soup, and moved on with my day.

The next day at my workplace, a co-worker announced, "I made a whole bunch of food yesterday, and I brought in the extra. Please check because I don't want to take it home. There's just way too much." Pregnant and always hungry, I immediately went to the kitchen to check out what she brought. She had brought *butternut squash soup*, one of my favorite soups ever. I was already emotional with all the hormones, but I almost cried. I came back out and told everybody, "Guys, she brought butternut squash soup, the best ever! Don't you guys want some?"

Everyone said they weren't huge fans of butternut squash and suggested I take it home. I literally had enough soup for a week. It felt like God was saying, *I got your soup. I got you.*

These random gestures of God's love are spread throughout the Bible too. When Jesus was presented at the temple as a baby, Simeon announces that Jesus is the Messiah[56]. Mary and Joseph didn't need Simeon to confirm that. God had already sent them angels to tell them that their son would be the promised Savior. At the same time, Simeon's presence was God's way of encouraging Mary and Joseph that their son was the Christ. It was also an encouragement to Simeon, who had been waiting to see the Messiah before he passed away. God gave Simeon a gift by allowing him to meet Mary and Joseph, and celebrate the miracle of Jesus Christ's birth.

At random moments, God's love can drop into your life in the most personal and seemingly random ways. He wants you

[56] Luke 2:25-35

to know, "I see you. I got you. I get you." He speaks of His love through those moments. As you open up to these different paths, you begin to develop your own unique language with God. You might notice that, for example, you dream a lot. Or maybe God has surrounded you with some wise counsel, and all you need to do is tune in. No one can put God in a box. When you are open to Him leading you, He will.

Just Start Talking!

If you don't ask, you can't receive. Even if you feel like God hasn't spoken much to you previously, remember: He wants to speak to you, and He will. The first step in communicating with God is to get used to talking to Him, and asking Him questions.

When I started to learn this muscle, I asked silly questions. I remember one day, I asked Abba what shirt to wear. It sounds so silly, and I knew it really didn't matter, but I just wanted to strengthen my relationship with Him, and practice listening, like I was having a conversation with a friend. After praying, my attention was caught by this purple shirt in my wardrobe. I thought, "Cool, I'm going to wear the purple shirt today." And—here's the crazy thing—because of the phrase on that purple t-shirt (EX-Liar), I ended up having a full conversation sharing the gospel with someone at my university because they asked me about the "random" shirt. God can work with anything! Your prayers don't have to be about huge life and death matters; just start asking, and most importantly, start listening.

ACTIVATION POINTS

- Write out the different ways God has spoken to you in the past in each of the areas listed. When you look for these occasions, you will probably find them. If you don't find an example from every category on the list, that's fine, but ask the question.

- What are some of the reasons you have hesitated listening for His leadership/voice in your life?

- Are these reasons based in truth?

- What is something you need God to give you direction on right now? Bring it to His throne and ask Him to give you insight and wisdom in this specific area. Try leaning in to at least 3 of these methods and listen for God's response.

Chapter 6

TIMING IS EVERYTHING

"There is an appointed time for everything.
And there is a time for every matter under heaven—"
Ecclesiastes 3:1

Timing is one of the biggest areas of uncertainty people face in their desire to obey Jesus. In many songs and statements of surrender, there is very little discussion on the importance of timing in what God has called you to do. We like to think that timing doesn't matter, that God will speak a word today, and we can do it in 10 years with the same level of effectiveness. However, when you understand that God cares about the timing of events, you will have a higher level of motivation to follow His leadership. I will share one personal story and a few Biblical examples to demonstrate.

Cascading Events

Cascading events are moments where God asks us to learn, or do something today, in preparation for tomorrow. Our willingness (or unwillingness) ends up affecting our ability to step into the next opportunity.

My second album, *Broken Spirit, Contrite Heart,* was a live recording and we had been preparing for it for a year. On the night of the recording, there was an accident on the highway that got it completely locked down. Our main producer got stuck in the gridlock and missed the entire event. As the leader, I had not anticipated that being a possibility, and had no back up person trained on our production process. In this circumstance, a volunteer who had shown up early was briefed on each track as people filled in.

As you can guess, the tracks were out of time, and the levels in our monitors were all over the place, to name a few things. While God moved powerfully in the live event, it was not a quality recording we could put in album form. It took us 2 years to re-record the live event, as we did not have the funds to pay someone else to do it. The producer felt truly remorseful and offered his studio for free, for however long it would take to re-create the album from scratch. The problem was, he was not available to do the studio work, so it was on myself and about 5 members of our team to learn how to produce an album. This meant, not only did we have to sing, play the songs and instruments again, but we needed to learn how to balance levels, overdub, edit, and equalize; we were all learning almost from scratch. This took us two years to complete because we still wanted to maintain a standard of excellence. We would not move on if it didn't sound right.

We bathed the process in prayer, gratitude and focus but one day I got upset – really upset. I was sitting at the workstation with the large monitors in front of me, staring at these tracks, and I started to complain. "God, how could this happen? This has literally put my life on pause for two years. Who would have guessed that one accident would cause us to still be here 2 years later? I don't even know how to produce. I'm not a producer, I'm a singer. An artist. This isn't my job!"

God spoke to me, "Toyin, if you wanted to learn how to produce an album you would have needed to pay a tuition of thousands of dollars. You would have taken years to get the degree in sound engineering and production. Meanwhile, you have been given unlimited free studio access to a space you do not own. You are able to make the album sound the way you would like, and have full creative control post-recording. Focus. Learn. Use this time wisely."

Noted.

I repented for my grumbling and got back to work with a renewed gratitude for this unique opportunity to learn. Instead of just clicking and moving along, I started to pay attention to what I was doing and learning in a more intentional way.

A year later, our not-for-profit had been chosen to create an anti-bullying song for the Boys and Girls Clubs of Canada (BGCC). Their administrator had coordinated with our team as well as 3 producers –other volunteers. People travelled from different parts of Ontario for the recording. When we arrived, we found out that the main producer along with the back-up producers weren't able to make it. After a few hours of trying to figure out what to do, the administrator told us they would have to cancel the recording and try to coordinate another day and time.

While it was a long shot, I asked them what software the recording studio used. It was Pro Tools, the same recording software we had been using for the last 2 years. We told them we could sing, and as a team also produce, since we were extremely familiar with Pro Tools. As I sat behind the glass in the booth recording my team members and friends, I couldn't help but thank God for His leadership and foresight. Not only did He teach us in time, but to help me notice the value, He corrected me, so I didn't miss the lesson because of my complaints. If I had skipped the lesson or tried to take shortcuts, it would have been clear to me that I had missed the opportunity to learn what was needed for that moment, in the studio with the BGCC.

Temptations With Timing

Often, we miss His instructions because we aren't asking about the timing. I've found that when we don't get clear on the *when*, we often delay doing the thing at all. Then, the when becomes never, and the never becomes disobedience. Sometimes, we have the opposite problem: instead of delaying, we jump the gun. In our human zeal, we step ahead of God into things that He hasn't told us to do yet. The temptation to act outside of God's timing can go either way.

Temptation 1: Delay

When I had just gotten serious about my walk with God, I received a lot of encouragement before working on my first album. I'd sung in churches for a couple of years, and had written songs. I often heard, "You should write. You should do an album," and I felt like it was something God wanted me to do.

I had excuses; I'm too young. I'd never done this before. I have no idea where to start. I don't know the right people. I don't have money. It's a crazy idea!"

It wasn't until my uncle told me that if I completed the album by December of that year, he would cover half of the costs. At that point, I said, "I can generate the other half. I'm going to get this album started."

Often, we need those nudges. But even with them, we can still ignore God's now timing. Once, a client of mine shared how he and his wife prayed for God to provide a down payment for a house. We had been working together for about a year, and I knew that they had been praying for this for a long time. He shared, "Toyin, you don't even know this, but we got the amount we needed for the down payment earlier this year. But we were so afraid of the monthly mortgage, we didn't get the house. Now that money is spent. We're back in the same place as before, asking the Lord to provide the down payment for a house."

God showed his faithfulness and mercy by providing the amount they needed again the following month. However, after that experience, they were determined not to make the same mistake twice.

Here's the thing about waiting too long: if you wait when God is saying go, there is such a thing as a missed opportunity. Yes, God works all things together for our good, and He's able to redeem some of those missed opportunities, but it's better to avoid that.

No matter where you are, there's always going to be a reason to delay or disobey. There's always going to be a reason to stay comfortable. You'll always be able to find an excuse. Listen to when God says move, and step out.

Stop Chasing Yesterday's Dream

Many try to finish the things God asked them to do when they hear a message like this even when it has become completely irrelevant. You do not need to pursue a dream God gave you 10 years ago if it is no longer applicable today. For example, if God gave you an idea for a website that would serve video store rentals, but those stores don't exist anymore. Own that it was an instruction you received 10 years ago that wasn't followed through on. Then, let go of what was, and seek the Lord today. Ask for His now word to you. You are no longer that version of yourself, and God has plans for you today that will be better than anything you can imagine if you are willing to follow Him, today.

God is Merciful, And Redeems The Time

It is often difficult to accept that there are missed opportunities that do not come back. There are consequences of missing God's timing. At the same time, He is merciful, and redeems the time, so we don't have to wallow in self-pity or regret about those lost opportunities or lost time.

I've watched people who missed opportunities hold themselves captive for years, allowing a mistake that God is able and willing to redeem become a foothold the devil has on their minds. They allow one missed opportunity to create 15 more instances of missed obedience, referencing their unfaithfulness in the past as a reason for their unworthiness to follow today.

Hear me clearly: While we aim for perfection as the Lord says[57], we also receive His forgiveness and mercy when we fall short. His kindness leads us to repentance.[58]

This means we recognize whatever held us back from obedience in the first place, and commit to move differently the next time; hit reset, and fiercely commit to pursue His will in our lives at this time.

Temptation 2: Trying To Hurry God Up

We can also be tempted to go outside of God's timing by jumping the gun. There are times where God speaks a word to us, and we get micro vision. We think, "God gave me a promise, so it needs to happen in the next month." If the promise doesn't come to pass in the next month, we start to doubt. We wonder if God really said it, or start to question all the circumstances and people involved. We need to develop a long term vision for God's will and purposes in our lives. Without a long term vision, we suffer from doubt and anxiety. Remember, the promises of God are yes and amen!

Give It Time

Imagine you plant a seed in a garden. You water it. You fertilize it. You make sure it's getting adequate sunlight. But

---

[57] Matthew 5:48

[58] Romans 2:4

when you check it a week later, you don't see any growth. It looks like nothing is happening.

So, let's say you uproot the seed from that spot. You decide the soil isn't good, and you're going to find better soil elsewhere. Now you give it a full month. A little green shoot starts to come up, but it's nothing like the big, impressive plant you'd been imagining. You uproot the plant again to find a "better" spot. You keep doing this and then start to wonder why the seed isn't thriving or producing fruit. It's because the seed hasn't gotten enough time to settle in. Roots, growth, and fruit take *time*.

When I started the business God told me to give it everything I had for ten years. He said, "you haven't done it until you've run for ten years," because He knew I had a tendency to want to move from one thing to the next. That was 2016. Within four years, I had gone from massively struggling, to becoming a millionaire and had seen thousands of people experience huge financial and life transformation through it. The business is still growing every year. I'm still showing up, and serving, alongside an amazing team. Often, one of the best ways we can obey God regarding timing is to give Him *enough* of our time.

Not All At Once

It's also important to understand that it may not happen all at once. In 2012, God gave me a vision for a worship ministry tour. I assumed that must include touring the United States. We contacted churches in the States. We booked tour dates in the States. Then one day, I was reading Acts 1:4-8, where Jesus gathered His disciples and, "Commanded them not to leave Jerusalem, but to wait for what the Father had promised... So, when they had come together, they were asking Him, saying, 'Lord, is it at this time You are restoring the kingdom to Israel?' He said to them, 'It is not for you to know times or epochs which the Father has fixed by His own authority; but you will receive power when the Holy Spirit has come upon you; and you shall be My witnesses both in Jerusalem, and in all Judea and Samaria, and even to the remotest part of the earth."

I felt the Lord pause me there. I meditated on verse four, where it says, "He commanded them not to leave Jerusalem." Then He just said to me, "Now is not the time for the States. I want you to reach out to your Jerusalem first." For us, our "Jerusalem" was Toronto. God was telling us to perform at different churches within our own city.

My response to this was, "But God, it would be so great to tour the States. We already have our map. We have it planned out. I already have locations. I know the churches to reach out to." We'd even gotten printed introductions, and pamphlets for these churches that I knew would be excited to have us. I said, "It would be amazing! It would work." And God just said, "No. You're going to start in your Jerusalem. You're going to lay your foundation here. Then you're going to go out. When it's time, you'll reach people in the States."

We did eventually end up visiting, and ministering in churches in the States and God was faithful to move. Even more, now, my business reaches thousands of people in the States every single year, but that outreach was done in His way. That's what I love about God's timing. He reveals and unfolds His plan through such personal conversations with us, but it's a conversation that can only be had step by step. The temptations to go outside of God's timing can be corrected by having these conversations with Him.

Timing and Making Practical Plans

I used to believe that plans were more likely to succeed when they were supernaturally given from God. For example if God told me the exact date to release an album, it would do better than if I simply set a date. What this meant was I would often take no action even when God had given me a direction, because I was waiting on a dream, prophetic word, or confirmation in some form.

What I learned is that you need to start moving. God can and will redirect you if you start heading in the wrong direction. You will not always see the full picture in the beginning. If you are waiting to understand completely before you take action, you will be waiting a long time. It's better to, "Trust in the LORD with all your heart and do not lean on your own understanding."[59]

You need to balance waiting for God's leading and taking personal initiative. And when you are walking closely with Him, He will lead you in slowing down, speeding up, changing track or starting over.

---

[59] Proverbs 3:5

Seasons

Seasons of life have a large impact on your focus; and they should. But many of us are so committed to our former selves, and former seasons that we suffer unnecessarily. We schedule our time for our past instead of our future.

I remember when my relationship with Joshua went from friendship to courtship, and we spent more time getting to know each other. I barely had time to sleep between personal prayer, ministry, service, my part-time job, counselling others, and finding time to connect and speak with him. I sent an SOS text message to two mentors– married women, with children, who were also involved in leading others– asking how they did it. I told them I felt like I was crashing. "I can't even think straight because I'm so tired. I can't imagine what I will do when we are married. I can't be married and not have time for my husband! What if I have children?" I was so stressed thinking about it, and the response of one of my mentors carried me through that season and every one after it.

She said, "Toyin, you are functioning in this season as if you are still a single woman. You're not. You need to get honest about the use of your time and cut things out. Stop counselling 3 hours a day. Schedule time to be with the one you love. All these people you are giving your time will likely not be around 30 years from now. He will if you get married. So invest the time in making sure this is the right choice." It set me free to let go of what was.

Each new season since, I have done the same. I have dedicated time to being present with the Lord. Then my husband. Then my children. Then ministry or clients once I got into business. We are often saying yes to so much else that fills our time which takes away the time we have for what matters most.

Obedience is extremely difficult if you are trying to do today's work while carrying the responsibilities from seasons' past. In every season, ask God what your primary focus is. It may be the same for 20 years, but be very clear so that you are focused on what is most important to Him in each season.

Sidenote: You are not the Messiah. It is not your job to fix everything and save everyone. As my dad once said to me, "There will always be an opportunity to serve and minister. You aren't missing anything by focusing now on something God has called you to do. When you are finished, there will always be more ministry work to be done."

Flexibility in Obedience

Obedience will teach you flexibility in timing. In 1 Samuel 13:5-14, Saul was a relatively new king to Israel and the Philistines had set up an attack against them. While it says the Philistines, "were as many as the sand on the seashore," Saul only had about six hundred men with him. Saul had been given clear instructions from God through the prophet Samuel to wait 7 days, until he (Samuel) came to make sacrifices to God. Saul waited 7 days, but Samuel didn't show up on time.

In his frustration and fear, Saul went ahead and made the sacrifices on behalf of the people, which crossed the line between his role as a king and the role of a priest/prophet. When Samuel arrived, he asked him, "What have you done?" Saul shared all his reasons and excuses, but Samuel said, "You have acted foolishly! You have not kept the commandment of the LORD your God, which He commanded you, for the LORD would now have established your kingdom over Israel forever."[60] Saul lost the kingdom because He thought God was "late" and decided to take things into his own hands.

A lack of flexibility in timing also opens the door to offense when we feel God isn't moving how we expected. In following Abba's leadership, here are a few principles that have helped guide my perspective on God's timing:

- I will be rewarded in eternity.[61]
- God's timing is not mine - 1,000 of my years are 1 day to Him.[62]
- God's thinking is not mine. His thoughts and ways are higher.[63]
- God is *always* right on time.[64]
- I will do what He said and trust Him with the results.[65]

In fact, there have been so many times when I have seen God fulfill His word after the time I expected, sometimes a month or a year later. And some of them, I have yet to see fulfilled. But I stay focused on His present word and do my part. Then trust Him with the fruit. You may ask how can I trust Him with these things? That's going to be the focus of the next chapter.

---

[60] 1 Samuel 13:13

[61] James 1:12, Matthew 16:27

[62] 2 Peter 3:8

[63] Isaiah 55:8-9

[64] Habakkuk 2:3

[65] Psalm 37:5, Jeremiah 17:7-8, Isaiah 26:3-4

ACTIVATION POINTS

- Have you had missed opportunities or moments where you acted outside of God's timing. What lessons did you learn from those experiences?
- Are there any areas in your life right now where you are delaying obedience to God's instructions?
- Do you find yourself rushing ahead of God's timing in certain areas? How does impatience impact your decision-making process?
- Take inventory of any dreams or goals from the past that you haven't pursued due to timing concerns or other reasons. Are these dreams still relevant to your current season of life? If so, what steps can you take toward them now?
- Think about instances where you may have missed God's timing and experienced feelings of regret or self-condemnation. Repent for them, accept God's mercy and move forward in obedience.
- Reflect on Toyin's analogy of planting seeds and the importance of allowing time for growth. Are you more focused on immediate results or on patiently nurturing growth over time? How can you apply this principle of patience and perseverance in your own endeavors?
- Examine your current season of life and the priorities that dominate your time and energy. Are there areas

where you need to realign your focus to better reflect God's purposes for this season of your life? What do you need to acknowledge in order to be more effective?

- Consider Saul's impatience and lack of flexibility in 1 Samuel 13. In what ways do you relate to Saul's struggle with timing and obedience? How can you apply these principles to your own life to avoid the pitfalls of impatience and inflexibility?
- Consider practical steps you can take to surrender your timing preferences to God and embrace His perfect timing for your life's journey.

Chapter 7

LEARNING TO
TRUST GOD

It's one thing to hear what God is saying and an entirely different thing to actually step out and do it. Trusting God is the foundation that helps us hear clearly, have confidence in His timing, and obey, especially when it feels scary, uncomfortable, or there is a risk of failure.

"God, I can't do this!"

At the beginning of my journey in obedience, God asked me to make a worship album with the songs He'd given me as I discovered His love. I was excited about that process even though it had stretched me outside of my comfort zone. Then, God had asked me to release the album through a concert. I thought it was a fantastic idea. I loved that I would get to share these songs He'd given me with members of my church and some friends from other churches. I practiced for months, hoping for the best; finally tickets to the concert were put up for sale.

A few weeks after the tickets were released, my mom excitedly told me, "We're sold out!" I was confused. We had printed 400 tickets, far more than I thought we even needed.

"What do you mean we're sold out?"

"All the tickets are sold, they're gone!" she said.

"Oh, wow! Great!" I was excited! There was more pressure to get it right, but I figured we could.

One Monday, shortly after the concert sold out, I went to a service on my university campus. A woman I had never met before was leading us in worship. In the middle of a song, her voice reached a stunning climax. It was so out of this world that I thought an angel had entered the room. My eyes popped open mid-song to check that this was a real human singing. I was in awe.

After worship, a young man stood up to share the Word and gave a powerful, deep revelation from a familiar Bible verse. I kept thinking, "How did I not see this? This dude is amazing. He hears from God!" I felt more awe at the presence of God in their lives. After the service, both of them came to me separately to let me know they had heard about my concert and had gotten tickets to attend. I should have been excited. Instead, I panicked.

I was supposed to sing and preach at this concert. That day, I found out that those two awe-inspiring individuals planned to attend, as well as a bunch of other singers and musicians I highly respected. These people were on another level entirely. How on earth could I even try to measure up?

That night I went to my bedroom, ready to have a conversation with Jesus. I was upset. I said, "Abba, you know I don't sound like her, not even close! I don't get revelations as deep as what he shared tonight. My voice is low and raspy. All the big worship leaders have high, angelic soprano voices." I felt trapped. It was too late to cancel, but there was no way I wanted to go on stage with them in the audience, and make a fool of myself. I continued on, "Why did you put me in this position? Why would you tell me to do the album when it doesn't compare to them? Why would you tell me to do a concert when you have people who could do it better? Why are you trying to embarrass me?" I wrestled in prayer for a long time.

Finally, God responded and all He did was ask: "Will you trust me?" Would I trust Him? Could I trust Him?

Often, when I don't know what to say to God, I sing my thoughts instead. So while still feeling the fear, I blurted out a new chorus as a response to His question:

> *"I give up, I let go. I submit myself to your will.*
> *In your Word, I will find my rest.*
> *I lay myself down at your feet Lord.*
> *I lay myself down at your feet Jesus."*

As I sang, I wept.

I didn't understand what He was doing. Jesus was asking me to do the scariest thing I had ever done in my life, at that point. I honestly didn't think I could do it, but I finally surrendered. I let go. And as I kept singing that phrase, I was able to get to a place where I remembered: *it's not about me.* It's about God. And if He called me to it, then who cares what they think about my voice.

"Alright Abba, I'm down. You are worthy. But please, please help me."

Know the One Who Calls You

I've heard people say, "I just don't know how to trust God," or "I hear you talk about surrendering to God, but I just can't do it." The truth is, every single person on this planet is a person of faith. The question is what is your faith placed in?

When you stand in front of your couch, you don't think twice about sitting down, leaning back, and letting go of your weight. You believe it will hold you up, because you trust that the couch has got you. When we get into a car that has gas and works, we don't think, "Oh man, how is this car going to get me to my destination?" We have faith that the car is going to take us where we need to go.

The reason many of us trust our chairs, cars, airplanes, and even the roof over our heads is because we have faith. If you are currently reading this book inside a home or building, you believe that structure can hold itself up without crashing down. We even fall asleep in these structures!

The reason we trust these things is because we can see them. Seeing makes it easy. People who find faith more difficult haven't gotten to *see* God for who He really is.

If you're going to live a lifestyle of joyful, radical obedience, you have to see who is calling you to the table. I'm talking about more than head knowledge. If you don't know who God is on a heart level, and trust Him, then you won't have confidence to do the things that scare you. Instead, you'll listen to that voice in your head that says, "You're not good enough. You don't have what it takes. You can't do this. You're going to fail. You're on your own." The voice of your own insufficiency is going to drown out the voice of your good Father.

He will call you to do the things that scare you—that's His specialty. When He does, it will be impossible for you to respond willingly and joyfully, if you don't have full confidence in His ability to care for you through it. Remember, it's not your ability (or inability) that's at stake; it's His grace. When you know God–and know what He is capable of—it becomes possible to trust Him. It allows you to obey Him with confidence, do it well, until the end, and obey Him with joy.

The more you see how God has shown himself to be constant and consistent in your personal life, the more your faith in him with increase. Trusting becomes easy.

Who is This God?

God is beyond what any of us can fully know or comprehend. He's unsearchable. You could search for billions of years, and there will always be more of God to learn about. Think of this like trying to comprehend the entire ocean. You could never know everything that's happening in each part, at every depth, or in every moment.

God is bigger than the oceans. He is bigger than the universe. He *created* all of it. But that doesn't mean we shouldn't try to know Him. We can stand at the shore and see the horizon. We can stand in it and feel the water's dampness and the power of the waves. We can dive in, and explore the world below the surface. In a similar way, we experience and begin to know God.

While we won't know everything about Him, growing in our knowledge of God in His word, His ways, and His character allows us to trust Him when He calls us to obey.

God is Good

The goodness of God anchors your obedience. The Bible talks about the goodness of God in more verses than I can name. One of my favorites is in Exodus, when Moses asks God to reveal Himself: "And the LORD passed before him and proclaimed, "The LORD, the LORD God, merciful and gracious, longsuffering, and abounding in goodness and truth…"[66]

Like Moses, we ask God, "Show me your glory. Show me who you are. I want to know you. I've seen you working. I've had conversations about you, but I want to *know* your character." Well, here we have God's answer. This was the moment in scripture when YHWH—the creator of the universe—decided to introduce Himself with words that aren't sufficient. And what does He say? That He abounds in goodness. And then it is repeated throughout scripture[67].

The reason you must intimately know the goodness of God is because the result of obedience is never guaranteed. Sometimes, things go better than imagined. Often, as you obey Him, you learn, you grow, you see results of that obedience. You *know* you're in the right place, and it's all working together. It feels amazing! However, that's not always the case. You could do

---

[66] Exodus 34:6

[67] For further reading, see Psalm 34:8, Psalm 100:5 and Nahum 1:7.

everything Abba tells you to do, do it to the best of your ability, and still not have the outcome you wanted. Many of us know the deep disappointment from feeling like you did your part only to have things turn out differently than you expected. The only way to continue showing up in the midst of hardship is if you believe that He works all of it together for your good.

Romans 8:28 says, "And we know that God causes all things to work together for good to those who love God, to those who are called according to His purpose." In Christian circles, we often throw this verse around like candy. It has become cliché. But we do not fully believe all things work together for our good, *because God is good.* Often, when we are disappointed, feeling God should have done things differently, it is because we believe "goodness" should mean that we never suffer. However, goodness doesn't relate to the comfort or ease of our circumstances. Goodness is God's ability to *carry you through* challenges.

Job is a great example. He goes through total breakdown. He loses seven children, all of his money, and his business. His friends turn against him, and even his wife questions his faith. As if that isn't enough, his health is attacked, and everything around him crashes down. What makes it worse, this man is actually faithful to God; someone that God was pleased with. God even mentioned him to the devil saying, "Look at my servant Job, look at how pleased I am with him."[68]

The devil brought destruction on Job to test his heart. Job could have turned completely away from God. He went through a deep grief, to the point of telling God, "I wish I was

---

[68] Job 1:8

never born." But in the middle of his profound grief, he wasn't pulled away from the truth of the faithfulness of God. The story ends with a powerful dialogue between Job and God, where Job sees God more clearly, in all His power. Job responds to this by saying, "I have heard of You by the hearing of the ear; But now my eye sees You;"[69] God ends up restoring Job completely and blessing him with greater abundance than he had before.

God is not to blame for the destruction caused by the enemy. Many people quote Job when he said, "The Lord gives and He takes away."[70] But God was not the one who brought those trials on Job. It was the devil who caused so much destruction in Job's life, though God allowed it.

Suffering is inevitable. We live in a fallen world –full of sin and brokenness, sickness and betrayal, disappointment, and death– where people treat each other in horrific and unfair ways. And those things break God's heart more than they break ours. It is the devil who comes "to steal, to kill and to destroy," but Jesus came that we may have "life and life more abundantly."[71]

If you want to know the goodness of God in the midst of disappointment, come to Him with a genuine desire to find Him. Don't try to filter out your hurt, pain, or pretend the disappointment isn't there. Instead, bring that hurt and pain to Him. Be real and raw with Him, and allow Him in. In every situation where you're disappointed, He wants t show you His

---

[69] Job 42:5

[70] Job 1:21

[71] John 10:10

goodness and to carry you through that time.

It might be tempting to avoid this conversation; in the hardest moments, your faith in the goodness of God might be so shaken that you don't want to approach Him with your pain. But, if you want to have an experiential confidence in the goodness of God, have the conversation with Him. *Especially* when things get really bad. Learn about His goodness through the ups and downs. When you open yourself up to God, everything that happens brings you closer to Him, instead of further away.

If you still question God's goodness in your life, hear this: He didn't have to offer mercy and forgiveness for our many sins and mistakes, yet that is exactly what He gives us. The Bible says that even when we were sinners—enemies of God—He became a man. He died on the cross. He took our place and accepted the punishment for our sins.[72] Jesus' sacrifice is the evidence of the goodness of God.

God is so good, in fact, that He didn't just give us mercy. He didn't just become a man and die on our behalf. He gives us grace to experience a relationship with a holy, pure, and righteous God. We get to call Him, "Abba, Father!" Hebrews 10:19 says, "We can boldly enter the throne of grace through the blood of our high priest." In the midst of a fallen and a broken world, be anchored by the fact that no matter what happens to you, God is good. He loves you, and He's got your back.

---

[72] Romans 5:8

God is Trustworthy

While I can easily trust my 7-year old daughter to help me put away our laundry, I wouldn't trust her to drive me home in an emergency. You can trust your dog to catch a stick when you throw it— but you wouldn't trust your dog to make dinner, because it isn't able to do that. You can only trust a person based on their capability.

God has *no* limits. There is no end to what He is capable of, which means we can trust Him with any and everything. If you are not *deeply* aware of His ability, you won't actually put your weight on Him. You'll continue shouldering burdens He is more capable of carrying than you. Understanding God can be trusted will transform the way you show up[73].

Over a decade ago, I was in a Bible study with friends. God asked me, "Toyin, if you had a Father who had all the resources in the world, all the wisdom, and all the power to do anything, and that Father freely shared those resources with you—how would you impact others?" That question changed my level of expectation of what God could do with my life. It transformed the way that I showed up to the tasks He called me to do because I could see Him more clearly. He is not sitting with his hands tied, hoping that we will make it through on our own. Our Father has unlimited wisdom, unlimited power, and unlimited resources to get anything He calls us to do, done. He has your back.

That night I shared this question with my friends, and we

---

[73] See 2 Samuel 7:28 (NIV), Psalm 19:7 (NIV), Psalm 111:7-8 (NIV), and Lamentations 3:22-23 (NIV).

LEARNING TO TRUST GOD

thought of some huge ways we could impact others positively. Over the years, we have watched each other live out those dreams we thought were completely impossible. God has no limits. He is capable of more than you can imagine.

> *"Blessed is the man who trusts in the Lord and whose trust is the Lord. For he will be like a tree planted by the water, that extends its roots by a stream and will not fear when the heat comes; but its leaves will be green, and it will not be anxious in a year of drought nor cease to yield fruit."*
> *Jeremiah 17:7-8*

God is Powerful

"Declaring the end from the beginning, And from ancient times things which have not been done, Saying, 'My plan will be established, And I will accomplish all My good pleasure.'" Isaiah 46:10.

God doesn't need permission from anyone to be and do what He chooses.[74] When He gives us a directive, He is not sitting back biting his nails. He is actively involved in the things He calls us to— changing hearts, opening doors, and fighting battles we often don't see.

When things look impossible, God has the power to create. He caused the sun to stand still in order for Israel to win a battle.[75] He spoke the world into existence.[76] Everything that

---

[74] Psalm 115:3

[75] Joshua 10:12

exists was made from the word of God. When God calls you to do something that no one that you know has done before, trust in His ability to create, change, affect hearts, and provide.

Trust Him to be God.

> *"All the inhabitants of the earth are of no account, But He does according to His will among the army of heaven and among the inhabitants of earth; and no one can fend off His hand or say to Him, 'What have You done?'"*
> *Daniel 4:35*

When you understand the power, reach, ability, and magnitude of the God who is calling you to the table, you show up differently. You take risks differently. You are able to move through moments that feel overwhelming because it doesn't matter if *you* don't have what it takes—because He does.

A.W Tozer said, "God is looking for people through whom He can do the impossible. What a pity that we plan only the things we can do by ourselves." If your plans do not require the power of God then are you really pursuing God-sized dreams? When you understand the omnipotence of God, you step into battles with a swag in your step. With confidence that nothing catches Him by surprise or overwhelms Him and because He is the captain of the army– you always win.

---

[76] Hebrews 11:3

God is Faithful

In 2 Timothy 2:13, the Apostle Paul writes, "If we are faithless, He remains faithful, for He cannot deny Himself." Even in the face of our weakness and failure, God is unchanging and faithful. God establishes covenants with His people and faithfully fulfills His end of the covenant, even when we fail to do so.[77] He always keeps His promises and remains steadfast in His love and commitment to His children.[78] It is His nature, and is not dependent on us.

The Bible says He's the same yesterday, today, and forever.[79] He is still doing the same things today that He did in the Bible thousands of years ago. He does not change His character, purposes, or promises. While people and things around us are always in flux, God's unchanging nature makes Him completely reliable.[80] Not only that, His will is perfect, and His plans for His people are for our good and not for harm.[81] Often we are so focused on the few moments when we feel God didn't show up in the way we expected, that we forget or overlook the many times He did.

By remembering His consistency in our lives, we have the faith we need to take risks. I invite you to think of your personal experiences of His faithfulness. Think about those moments where you felt backed up against a wall, and somehow, He brought you through.

[77] Genesis 15:18, Deuteronomy 7:9

[78] 1 Corinthians 1:9

[79] Hebrews 13:8

[80] Malachi 3:6, Hebrews 13:8

[81] Romans 12:2, Jeremiah 29:11

In order to comprehend and trust in the faithfulness of God, you have to remember you are surrounded by broken and imperfect people. They promise things, and don't deliver. Maybe you've been told one thing, while they did something different. Maybe people failed to follow through on their word. Friends may have left in the moments where it counted, or siblings turned against you. Our world is full of broken promises, and we are tempted to associate God with the unfaithfulness of people around us. Even the people who love us the most may break their word at one point or another, whether they intended to or not, simply because they are human.

In order for you to trust the faithfulness of God, you have to separate Him from your experience with people. Accept that your logical brain just cannot understand His level of stability and consistency. Find Him in His Word. He is more consistent than the sun! He sets the sun's schedule. Even if the sun were to retire, God would remain faithful. Our rational minds don't have a reference for eternal faithfulness from our social contexts or from the people who love us the most.

> *"God is not a man that He should lie, nor a son of man, that He would change His mind. Has He said, and will He not do it? Or has He spoken, and will He not make it good?" - Numbers 23:19*

God's faithfulness doesn't always come packaged the way you might expect. When God called Noah to build a boat, He told him that rain would fall and flood the earth. Just one little sidenote - the people of Noah's generation had never seen rain. The earth had been fed water by a mist that came up from the ground.[82] Still, Noah had faith in God's Word even though he had never seen rain before. He started to build a structure that seemed completely unnecessary; something that had never been created before. This boat (ark), was to be large enough to hold animals of all kinds.

It also didn't take him a year or two. Scholars say it took him 55-75 years to build the ark.[83] Can you imagine how many people likely laughed at Noah in those 55 *years*? How many people saw this old man carrying wood, constructing layer after layer, creating cubbies for animals? He *was* the crazy guy who "heard a voice" tell him that there was going to be a flood when they had never even seen rain. *He was crazy until he wasn't.* When the first few drops began to fall, it was too late to join him and his family. Because of Noah's faith in God's word, his family was saved when the flood came, and the Word of God came to pass.

You grow in the knowledge of God's faithfulness by trusting and obeying. In this way, you co-create circumstances where He gets to step in and show Himself as faithful; not just for fun, but for His glory. The more you do this, and see Him show up, the greater your faith grows. Even if you don't understand the conclusion, you learn that He knows what He's doing.

I can't give you a deep, experiential, heart-level acceptance of the faithfulness of God. I can only show you through the Bible, and personal stories from my own life, and those of people around me. But make no mistake, you can experience it too.

---

[82] Genesis 2:5-6

[83] https://answersingenesis.org/Bible-timeline/how-long-did-it-take-for-noah-to-build-the-ark/

God is Just and Merciful

The Bible speaks of God's abundant love and compassion toward His creation. His love motivates Him to act in ways that are just and merciful.[84] God never overlooks injustice, and He constantly gives us opportunities for redemption. Why is it important to understand that God is just? Because when you truly open your hearts to this experiential walk with Him, you're going to have to do it with *people.* And people are broken. All of us have been hurt, and have hurt others. If you're reading this book, there is a 100% likelihood that you've been hurt by people. It might feel hard to fully trust that God has your back because of this. Understanding the principle of His justice frees you to trust Him. He hates when we hurt each other, and He will fight to defend the hurting.[85]

> *"The Lord will maintain the cause of the afflicted, and will execute justice for the needy." Psalm 140:12*

For you to truly, freely, and joyfully obey God, you will have to *forgive* those who hurt you because offense always hinders His call on your life. It grows into bitterness, anger, and can completely derail your walk of obedience. You become reactive to others, and protective in areas where He calls you to be expansive.

Holding onto the baggage of unforgiveness while trying to do what God's calling you to do is like trying to fly a kite with a hundred-pound backpack; you can't do it. The flying of the kite

---

[84] Psalm 136:26, Lamentations 3:22-23

[85] See Romans 12:19 and Isaiah 30:18.

becomes a punishment instead of fun, something you dread. What should feel like freedom becomes a burden. In order to forgive, you can rely on the fact that God doesn't take your pain and experience lightly. He hates injustice and will return to make all the wrong things right. God's invitation for you to forgive is an acknowledgement that you can give your pain and hurt over to Him.

When you are confident in the justice of God, you get to let go of all the hurt, pain, and the baggage that would otherwise slow down your obedience to Him. You can trust that every act of sin has already been accounted for on the cross of Jesus Christ, or will be accounted for on the judgment day.

When I was first learning how to walk in obedience, I had come out of a complicated relationship where there was a lot of hurt and betrayal. I prayed, but found it almost impossible to forgive some of the people that were a part of the drama. I knew I wasn't free because each time I would hear one of their names even in passing, my heart's reaction would remind me that I hadn't let go of what happened.

If I'm being honest, when it came to one person, there was a part of me that wanted God to acknowledge how much this person had "destroyed" my life. I felt it was unfair or unjust to be expected to simply forgive him after everything.

But God kept bringing me back to this. As I was trying to understand how to let go in a genuine way, He directed me to read the book of Nahum. The central theme of the Book of Nahum is God's judgment and vengeance against the Assyrian Empire, particularly Nineveh, for its cruelty, violence, and oppression of other nations, including the Israelites. As I read the book, I saw the way God fights injustice and those who oppress His children, and it was serious. God doesn't play. Nahum 1:6 says, "Who can stand before His indignation? Who can endure the burning of His anger? His wrath gushes forth like fire, and the rocks are broken up by Him."

God does not ignore injustice. He reminded me that there is a real punishment for anyone who has sinned, and does not trust in Him as their Savior. When I finished reading the book, God asked me, "So, is this what you want for him?" I responded, "Well, no, I don't want it to be that extreme. I don't want him to be paying the price for his sin for eternity. I just want you to slap him on the wrist a little." God said, "Toyin, it's either full forgiveness for him through the cross of Jesus Christ, just like you have received, or he will have to pay the full punishment for all of his sin. Is that what you want?"

When the gravity of God's punishment for our sin hit me, I began to pray for the very person who had deeply hurt me. I prayed that he would come into the saving knowledge of Jesus Christ–like I had–and be completely forgiven, not just for hurting me, but for all of his sin.

I reached out to him and shared the gospel with him. He responded, "Toyin I don't need any of this, I am already a Christian." I tried to explain to him that we both thought we were Christians because we were born into church culture, but from our lives we definitely didn't have a relationship with God. He rejected what I had to say.

I called him a few times over two years with the same message. Eventually, he told me that God had spoken to him and he had dedicated his life to God. I asked him about the parts of his lifestyle that we knew didn't glorify God. He shared how God had convicted, changed and transformed him. Based on major life decisions he had made, I could tell it was real. I got off the phone and thought, "His sins are now on the cross." It felt bittersweet, knowing he would never pay the punishment for hurting me, but I also rejoiced that Jesus bore the punishment for what had happened. We were now both free. Thank God!

Forgiveness does not negate actions you may need to take to protect yourself or others who are vulnerable around you. You can forgive a person, and pursue justice through the courts if it is a legal matter. For example, if a child has been molested, you can report the matter to the police. You can aim to stop it and make sure the person cannot harm another. At the same time, you can receive healing and forgive the person, so that you are completely set free.

When God asks you to trust and obey Him by forgiving others, it's not because He overlooks justice, or because the pain doesn't matter. He wants you to start this relationship with Him by letting go of the baggage. It has been taken care of on the cross of Jesus Christ, or it will be taken care of when Jesus returns. And if that person that has hurt you does not know Jesus, I invite you to pray for them. Pray that their sin and mistakes— just like yours— would be covered by the blood of Jesus, through the justice and mercy of God.

God is Wise

When you start to understand the depths of God's wisdom, you will find a bulletproof foundation for trusting Him. When He calls you to levels of leadership, creativity, and innovation–that you have never experienced and have no precedent for–remember that "there is nothing new under the sun."[86] God has seen it all already. He is omniscient, meaning He knows all things. His perfect knowledge ensures that His guidance and decisions are always wise and trustworthy.[87]

The Holy Spirit has lived inside of national administrators, artists, kings and queens, inventors, musicians, business owners, architects, and others, long before you entered the scene. And just like He gave them all wisdom to accomplish their tasks– long before the invention of the internet– He is able to give you the wisdom you need. He is the source of all wisdom and you can anchor yourself in Him.

I often pray, "God, move through me beyond my education, experience, and beyond my training. Abba, do what I can't do; do what only you can do. You have this experience. You have this expertise. It doesn't matter what I know or don't know. You are my source of wisdom."

Many people want to see 100 percent of what is expected before they obey God. What they don't understand is that there is *always* uncertainty. You don't know what you don't know, and you find out the inadequacy of your own wisdom very quickly when you step out in faith. Remember, the same God who calls

---

[86] Ecclesiastes 1:9

[87] Psalm 139:1-4

you to obedience knows *how* to get it done. There is a level of wisdom available to you in Christ Jesus that is beyond your own.

Often in business, music, politics or other endeavors, I get to a place where it truly feels like there is no good solution; no win-win. I feel stuck. At these times, I will often come to the Lord in prayer. He *always* gives wisdom that is beyond my thinking. I've seen the supernatural wisdom of God displayed too many times to count.

For example, my business team had a tough decision to make and I felt absolutely stuck. Someone wasn't doing well in her role. Let's call her Yolanda. We loved Yolanda, and she loved our team and mission. We didn't want her to leave, but for the longest time, God was saying, "You need to change things." I was stuck in the way we had always done things, and didn't know how He wanted me to change. I couldn't think of how else to make it work. I let her stay in that position even though it began to have a negative impact on the team, and mission overall.

Finally, in prayer I made the decision to trust God, even if it meant we would have to let Yolanda go. Within 24 hours, in a conversation with a couple of friends, I mentioned my challenge with Yolanda. "She's amazing," I told my friends. "We want to keep her, but I don't have another role in my business, and it's not working in her current role, so I'm considering letting her go." One of my friends said, "It sounds like she would be skilled at doing a role that we just created in our business."

As she began describing this new position she had created in her company and how it had served them, I recognized she was describing a need in our business that I had given up on long before. And as she detailed the qualities that a person would need to do that job well, she was listing Yolanda's exact attributes. In that moment, I realized that we could create the same position in my business which would address a pressing need, and align beautifully with Yolanda's skills. It was the exact solution that I needed. It just "came out" of a conversation, but really, it came out of trusting God enough to let go of doing it my way. Once I opened myself to His wisdom on this subject, no matter what it would've been, He ushered me into the conversation I needed to hear.

What's more? God's wisdom is good. It's not wisdom that overlooks or pulls people down. It is a wisdom that causes win-win situations for those involved. It is a wisdom that He offers to anyone who asks, which brings life wherever it goes.[88] *This* is the God that asks you to do what you've never done before.

> "But if any of you lacks wisdom, let him ask of God, who gives to all generously and without reproach, and it will be given to him."
> James 1:5

Learning the Language of Surrender

When I agreed to do my first concert despite the fear I felt, it wasn't a rah-rah, high energy moment. It was just accepting that He had called me to do this. I love Him, I wanted people

---

[88] See Romans 11:33, Jeremiah 33:3 and Proverbs 2:5-7.

to know Him; if this was what He wanted from me, then I was down. I was all in.

On the night of the concert, I remember how scared I felt, right up until start time. My heart was pounding out of my chest as I saw all the people go in. This was the first time I put myself out there in front of so many people and I was nervous; but the team had rehearsed and was very prepared.

When we began to worship, I forgot about talent, and gave everything I had before our King. I sang and shared from my heart, and God showed up beyond what I could have imagined. So many people came to know Jesus that night. People were set free from being oppressed in their minds. It wasn't just a concert. By the end, more people were at the front of the hall, and in the aisles praying for one another. Some were laying on the floor under the power of God, others were singing, dancing and worshiping. The presence of God was overwhelming.

God knew what the four hundred people who were attending the concert needed, and it was more than songs and words. It was the liberating power of His presence. When we learn to trust God—this good, trustworthy, powerful, faithful, just, and wise God—we are able to step out in obedience and we become other people's answer to prayers.

> *When you step out in obedience,*
> *you become the answer to other people's prayers!*

You can try to obey God without faith, but it won't please Him. Why not? Because when we obey without faith, we forget to seek God's wisdom or power, which means our efforts often don't produce fruit. Then we grow bitter. So, instead of experiencing life-giving obedience that multiplies fruit, draws people in, and shows them how amazing God is— we have become people who make it look hard, and are now jaded. We make it look like it sucks to walk with God.

That was me, early in my walk. When I first would obey God, I suffered through it. In fact, I thought it was *good* to suffer through it and I would learn more by suffering. But there was no joy. I was trying to obey out of my own strength and burning myself out. When you choose to be intentional about growing in faith, and expressing your love for God, you're able to learn the language of surrender. You start to let go of your preconceived notions of how things need to be, and what your life needs to look like. You learn the ability to distinguish what people expect from you, versus what God is calling you to.

If we're going to obey God in a way that pleases Him, it's not just about doing the right thing; it's about doing it in the *right way*. Trust the Word of God for what it is. Trust God for who He is.[89] Let Him do the heavy lifting. You can't do a God-sized dream in your own strength. If you could, it wouldn't be a God-sized dream! Faith and love give us the foundation to obey God with joy. And then if things do not work out the way you expected, that foundation of faith will carry you through.

---

[89] See Psalm 37:5 (NIV) and Proverbs 3:5-6 (NIV).

ACTIVATION POINTS

- Which of the attributes of God in this chapter most anchor you in trusting Him? Why?
- Write down ways God has shown Himself faithful in your life. Include times when you felt God's faithfulness, even though you faced personal failures or challenges.
- How does understanding God's unchanging nature impact your trust in Him during times of change and uncertainty? Relate this to Hebrews 13:8.
- How can you balance the call to forgive with the pursuit of justice in your own life and relationships? How does Romans 12:19 help in this balance?
- How can you actively seek God's wisdom in areas of your life where you lack experience or knowledge? How does God's promise in James 1:5 help you pray?
- What is one area in your life where God might be calling you to step out in faith, even in the face of fear or uncertainty? Where is God asking you to trust Him more?
- Can you think of an instance in your life where your faith grew as a result of obeying God, even when you didn't fully understand the outcome? Consider the example of Abraham's faith in Genesis 22 when he obeyed God's command to sacrifice Isaac.
- Have you experienced a situation where your obedience to God led to the liberation or transformation of others?

Chapter 8

FALLING FACE FIRST

I wish I could tell you that when you choose to obey God wholeheartedly, doors are always open for you, your path is always clear, and you get to ride into the sunset reflecting on only victories, blessings, and favour that chased you down in the journey. But that would be a lie.

At times you will feel like you did everything right and still got hit upside the head. You are following God's lead, doing the thing that scares you, only to find yourself in the pit of disappointment. It's hard. It's messy, and sometimes even confusing. Your ability to handle falling face first determines your ability to obey God today, and for decades to come; to stay until the end.

An inability to handle disappointment is often what takes people out of their commitment to obey God. It's helpful to prepare your heart for those unexpected twists and turns, which allow you to be more grounded in the process.

Knowing what to do when you fall face first helps you strengthen your ability to hear His voice. Each twist and turn becomes an opportunity to fine tune and learn to trust Abba even when it is difficult. But more than that, these moments are an opportunity to discover the grace and strength of the Lord. It's an opportunity to learn what love really looks like, and to uncover the hidden blessings God has for us even when it doesn't follow the standards of men. This creates deeper levels of trust and unwavering obedience.

Dealing With Disappointment

While there are so many incredible stories of God's leadership, His miraculous breakthroughs, and big turnarounds in my life, I've also felt the deep disappointment from wondering why things didn't work out despite following God's leadership. Let me share one of those stories with you.

I ran politically for a 3rd time, because of my passion to be a voice for the vulnerable, and for fiscal prudence. In my first campaign, I had an amazing trajectory. I won the federal candidacy, and was one of the only black female candidates federally, after an intense and extremely competitive nomination. I lost to a 25-year entrenched candidate who had represented the area for over 20 years.

Back at home, on the night we lost, my husband sat beside me on our bed, and said, "Toyin, I know you've had to keep it together for everyone tonight. Now we're home, it's just you and me, how are you feeling right now?"

After some reflection I responded, "I can feel God smiling on me. He asked me to run, and I can honestly say that I gave this campaign everything." We delayed the timing of our wedding so that it would not conflict with the nomination, and stayed in the country for our honeymoon. I was out door knocking almost every morning until nighttime and continued with that level of dedication even when I found out we were pregnant during the campaign. I knew that I knew that I had 'left it all on the field'.

He asked, "Are you sure? Is there anything else?" And I confirmed, "No babe, I literally feel the joy of the Lord all over us right now."

Second Campaign

The second time I felt God led me to run politically, we had recently moved to a new area and we barely knew anyone. I threw myself into serving the community in different ways, and went from having one friend to connecting with hundreds of people in a few months. I also sold the highest number of memberships for the party I represented, despite rumors, accusations, and intense opposition which included being up against 3 men who had been there for decades.

The day the vote took place, I learned a lesson about obedience that has impacted me ever since. As I mentioned, we had sold the highest number of memberships so it appeared that I had the momentum to win. I noticed that quite a few friends hadn't shown up to vote. When I called, they mentioned that a bunch of them were headed to a Christian conference, which was happening two towns away from the voting location. They said, "Toyin, God is with you! You are doing so well! We have prayed for you and know that you've got this in the bag." I said to them, "You need to come and vote! We didn't get this far for you to not show up! Jesus is at the voting booth today, not just at the worship conference," but they insisted, and of course I let them go on their way. Others couldn't make it because they needed to do groceries. Some weren't feeling well that day. And many other excuses often followed with reminders that God had my back, and there was no chance I could lose after all the work we had put in.

We finalized the voting period and when the count began, I won the popular vote (the highest number of votes among the four of us). However the voting system was not based on winning the popular vote. It was based on staggered voting, where the person with the lowest number of votes would be withdrawn, and their ballots would be redistributed among the remaining candidates. So, the last person out of us four was "dropped" and his votes were redistributed. He had told his supporters to support the other guys, so most of his votes went to the other two men. In fact, all three of my opponents did this. That was fine, as we won again with the most votes even after the distribution. However, when the second man was dropped from the ballot, and his votes were redistributed — between myself and my final opponent – most of his votes went to my opponent. I lost the entire nomination by 11 votes after winning the popular vote twice.

When people heard the final results, they were shocked. They didn't understand how I could have sold the most membership, had the most momentum, won the popular vote twice, but lost on the last ballot by 11 votes. The calls started to come in. Many of the people who couldn't make it for many reasons called to share their deep contrition for missing the vote.

This taught me that you can hear the word of the Lord,

you can hear prophecies, and pray many prayers, but if you do not show up and take action, those words will not take place. God will not apply for those jobs that He has spoken over you. He will not market your business by creating your social media account and posting on your behalf. He will not vote for you in your nation's election. He will do His part but you must do yours.

While I was disappointed and truly surprised by this loss, I was consoled by the fact that I could solely focus on my family and our growth. This experience had taught me such a valuable lesson about the need for personal and corporate action, and partnership with God.

Third Campaign

The third campaign was different. I was extremely hesitant to put myself out there again. In the previous two campaigns, I was doing ministry, and working in the not-for-profit sector before running politically. The third time, I was coming from a business background. In both my community work and my business, I was surrounded by people who were deeply grateful for the work we did in helping to make their lives better.

I knew that agreeing to run politically was like choosing to step into a boxing ring; people are willing to lie and say hateful things about you, without knowing you at all. There was constant conflict even if you didn't think of others from a competitive standpoint. For many, being associated with a particular party meant you represented "the other side". I truly did not enjoy politics. However, I wanted to be a voice for the everyday

Canadian, whose backs were breaking under the policy decisions being made. So, I decided to run again.

Once again, I outsold all my opponents, got the highest number of memberships in multiples, and once again, I lost. But this time, I was crushed. I had been personally attacked more than any of the other campaigns. People had started rumours about me. I witnessed a ridiculous amount of "politicking" and alliances. I had a naive belief that 'people who break the rules never win,' so seeing the outcome felt as though God was allowing the wicked to prosper.

I was so disappointed by this loss that I didn't notice I had stopped praying like I normally do. I decided to travel to the Dominican Republic for a vacation, after 2 years of running hard between the campaign, and my business. While on the trip, a friend of mine called. We normally ask each other what we're learning from the Lord. She started telling me how sweet the presence of God had been to her during that season. As she spoke, my heart was stirred up. I wanted to get back in relationship and conversation with Him. I looked for my Bible, and remembered that for the first time ever, I had left my Bible at home because I just didn't care to pray. Wow.

This underscores the importance of community. At that time, the state of my heart was very cold, and what allowed me to notice was a conversation with someone else with a burning heart.

I used my phone in the meanwhile, but could not wait to get home so I could hold my paper bible and be alone with Him. As soon as we returned, I asked my husband if I could take a working day to be alone with the Lord, and if he could help with the children. He agreed.

After 4 weeks since my loss, I finally brought my heart before the Lord. I sat on the bed with my journal on my lap. I was so heartbroken I had no words. Before I could say anything, I felt Abba say, "I've missed you, welcome back."

I still had no words. He said, "There is nothing you can't ask me. There is no emotion you can't bring to me. Nothing is too much for me to handle. Let's talk."

This was exactly what I needed. I was free to pour out my disappointment: the level of faith I had held on to, the financial and personal sacrifices we had made, the energy it had taken from me to stay in the campaign despite the hostility that had been sent my way, the compounding effect of all the unmet expectations–all of it.

"Why did you have me run again to have me lose again?"

"Why have me give money, time, and a ridiculous amount of energy for what feels like nothing?"

"Where do I go from here? I've lost so much momentum in the business over the last 11 months."

And He spoke.

He showed me how our personal lives had increased despite the ridiculous pressure we faced. He invited me to forgive the people who had attacked me personally.

He invited me to serve the person who won, and show love despite how I felt.

It was a difficult season, but the top priority was that my heart would stay soft, and I would avoid falling into bitterness.

He showed me all the ways the entire process worked for us and then accelerated my business beyond what I could have planned in my own wisdom. It was as if no time had been lost. He then showed me that this was the best opportunity I had received to learn to love well; to learn to love those I felt had attacked me. It was an opportunity to forgive them, even if it meant praying for and blessing them daily, until my heart did not react with pain or negativity when I thought of them. By the end of it, I was able to pray for them, and assist them in their campaigns and other projects, without carrying a chip on my shoulder. I was set free. The feeling of being able to come out of that season with a clear heart was one of the best feelings of my life. I knew that it was the fruit of God's work on my heart and that was a source of joy.

But... Where is God?

When things don't go as planned, you may also struggle to understand where God is in the story like Mary and Martha did when Jesus showed up late for their brother. The devil, also known as the accuser of the brethren, will often step in trying to accuse God and tell you that He has abandoned you. That you were foolish for trusting in Him.

Here's the truth that will strengthen your obedience: God is your strength in the fire. He is the reason you make it through the difficulty of disappointment.

One thing I teach our clients in the Self Mastery Academy is that everyone will be disappointed. Everyone will struggle and have challenges. We can either choose our challenge, or let life give it to us randomly.

I would rather learn how to navigate disappointment and challenges, knowing I am in the center of God's will, than navigate disappointment and challenges while living life for myself, and on my own.

Another thing I have noticed about these seasons is that God will often allow the disappointment to draw us closer to Him as we seek understanding and comfort. He is in this for the relationship. That willing heart that seeks Him for Him, and not for things or results; the heart that wants to know His ways, and not just His acts. We come to Him with our questions, and He draws us in more closely.

Handling the Emotional Fallout?

Let's be honest, dealing with disappointment can be emotionally taxing. Sometimes you wrestle with feelings of discouragement, frustration, or even anger toward God. Even Jesus was aware of the temptation for disappointment to create offense in our hearts. When John the Baptist sent his disciples to ask Jesus if He was the one they waited for, or if there would be another Messiah, Jesus highlighted all the miracles that had taken place as proof, but then added, "And blessed is any person who does not take offense at Me."[90] He knew that if John had a set idea of what the Messiah was supposed to do, he could be offended if Jesus moved differently from that expectation.

So how do you process these emotions and find peace amidst the disappointment? Here are the things I do in those moments:

---

[90] Matthew 11:2-6

Test The Word

I start by checking why I believe what I believe[91]. It will either be that I heard from the Lord, –and need to stand in faith and continue to take action– or that I missed it and need to recalibrate.

Don't be too committed to your own perspective of how things should have happened, and what you believe God said, especially when God is *refining* what was heard. Our inflexibility ends up wasting weeks, sometimes even years, and steals the 'now' word of the Lord. It is imperative that you fight fiercely for the word of the Lord you have received, while constantly testing yourself to ensure you are hearing what it is He is saying today.

Take Responsibility, Forgive and Repent

I check for, and repent for any actions I did not take to fight for the promise that God gave me.[92] I take responsibility for things that I did not do within my realm of responsibility.

I forgive and release any others who I feel may have impacted that outcome. For example, when doing full-time ministry, it's easy to feel frustrated about other believers not supporting the vision and/or mission. This is especially true when the work is not receiving the funding it needs, but you may be leading it unable to work additional hours. I have seen instances where the gap in financial support actually limited the vision that God had given the person. In cases like these, you want to be careful not to

---

[91] 1 Thess. 19-21
[92] 1 Timothy 1:18

develop a bitter or offended heart regarding those you feel could have provided more support.

Maybe it's not ministry. Maybe it was being fired unexpectedly when you had given your best years to an organization; seeing others cut corners and being blessed while your labor was ignored. It is mission critical that you keep your heart soft, and your love on.

Step Into Gratitude

If you want to obey God for the long haul, learn how to find a way to win in every situation. This helps me to see God's amazing hand at work while others only see failure.

Here's a practical exercise. Take out your notebook and reflect on a particular situation that created disappointment related to trusting God and walking in obedience. Now, sit down and make a list of the following:

1. All the ways God fought for you in the trouble you were in.

2. How He showed up on your behalf.

3. Practical breakthroughs you received from it. (e.g. I would never have done/have ___ if that didn't happen). How did God birth life out of death?

4. Your top lessons from that situation. What are some things that God was trying to tell you? How did He grow your maturity?

Recalibrate as Needed.

This is the final step in rebounding from disappointment when obeying God. Learn to let go; release and reset. Remember that a relationship with God is dynamic and not static. Listen in for what He is saying to do today, and go and do that.

Stop holding on to the past if the situation can no longer be modified. If there is a portion of responsibility that is needed, or there is still action for you to take in that area of obedience, then go ahead and get it done.

Failure Strengthens Character

Disappointment is the InstaPot® of character formation. When you face deep disappointment, you often see what's really in your heart; what you really wanted, or what you were afraid of.

What's the best way to get over the fear of what other people think? How can you be easily cured from the need to know what happens in the future? The answer is the same: allow yourself to fail.

It will help you build resilience. You also learn how to overcome the approval and rejection of people. You realize they will always have an opinion, and their opinions do not matter compared to God's perspective of your life. The places of hopefulness, endurance, joy, resilience–these virtues–all grow stronger with practice, like muscles; that's why they're the fruits of the Spirit, and not the gifts of the Spirit.

That's why you can't just be "gifted" the virtue of patience. Patience is a muscle. You have to work on patience. And the only way you can work on patience is by waiting. Waiting sucks. But in the middle of the wait, we learn how to be content - if we are intentional in our waiting.

Once while I read about the fruits of the Spirit in Galatians 5:22-23, the Lord highlighted the fruit of long-suffering. Abba said to me, "Toyin, do you know the definition of long suffering?" I said, "Abba, what is it?" He said, "It means, loooooooooooooooooooooooooooooo..." and He just kept going, "...ooooooooooooooooooooooooooooooooooong suffering. It goes past what you think you're capable of. If it didn't, you wouldn't need my Holy Spirit to develop that fruit."

For example, Samuel prophesied that David would be a king. He anointed him as Israel's true king when he was a young man. Still David had to wait seventeen years before he finally took the throne. In those seventeen years he was on the run, defending himself from a king who hunted him down unjustly. But God did come through.

Anyone who doesn't know God can be happy and nice when they get what they want. But it takes the work of the Spirit of God to be just as joyful in the twentieth year of waiting as you were on day four. In your seasons of deepest disappointment, you get to witness the faithfulness of God despite the brokenness of the world. God is faithful, and He takes care of His children.

> *"After you have suffered for a little while, the God of all grace, who called you to His eternal glory in Christ, will Himself perfect, confirm, strengthen, and establish you."*
> **1 Peter 5:10**

ACTIVATION POINTS

"Experience is not the best teacher, evaluated experience is the best teacher", John Maxwell.

Let's evaluate some of your more challenging experiences and see the gifts that God placed even there for you. Think about a situation that seemed like it had a negative impact on your life. Ask yourself the following questions.

- What did I learn from this experience?
- How have I grown or changed for the better because of this situation?
- Who supported me through that time, and how can I thank them?
- Can I identify any positive changes in my priorities or values because of this experience?
- Are there new opportunities that have arisen as a result of this challenge?
- How can I use my experience to help or inspire others?
- What strengths did I discover in myself?
- What can I be grateful for right now?

Chapter 9:

QUESTIONS IN
THE FIRE

While there is always tremendous growth from challenging seasons–before the breakthrough, before the understanding that hindsight provides–there are often questions we have in the midst of the fire.

Wondering whether you misheard or misinterpreted what God said is one of the first questions people have when things do not turn out as they expected. Doubt creeps in, and we question whether we accurately discerned God's instructions. However, something producing a different outcome does not mean that you did not hear what He said. Sometimes you did hear the word of the Lord, but specific factors affected its outcome.

Human Free Will

One significant factor is human free will. You have the ability to make choices that either align with or deviate from God's plan. This can affect the outcome of the prophetic words that have been spoken over you, or the situation you are in. In fact, sometimes other people's decisions and free will can also have an impact on a prophetic word that is spoken which concerns you. Like in my example with the second campaign.

Sin and Disobedience

Further to free will, if you choose to live in unrepentant sin, or you choose to live in condemnation, these things can create a barrier between you and God. This may cause you to hide in shame like Adam and Eve did in the garden, which stops you from hearing His direction and following it.

Sin can only keep us from seeing the fruit of obedience when we allow it. You take away that power from sin when you follow 1 John 1:9 which says, "If we confess our sins," that God is, "faithful and righteous, [and] will forgive us our sins and cleanse us from all unrighteousness."

Conditional Prophecies

A lot of prophetic words God gives –whether written in the Bible or spoken to you– are conditional on certain actions or responses. If the conditions specified in that word are not met, the outcome may look different from what was initially prophesied. So ask yourself, what was the context of that prophecy? What were the areas of application that were subjective?

Spiritual Warfare

I have noticed, especially in western Christianity, we can be lackadaisical about the warfare that takes place in the heavenlies over the words that God has spoken over our lives[93]. Yet the bible clearly states that the devil is not a passive bystander to God's call over you. He tries to delay or hinder the work of God. Thankfully, greater is He who is in us than he that is in the world[94]. Yet most Christians abdicate our authority, and end up carrying the consequence of spiritual attacks. While they could have pushed back against that assault through targeted prayer and fasting, and taken the victory. I'll share more on this in Chapter 10 - Holy Spirit Your Wild Card. There are also entire books devoted to this topic of the Believer's authority. I have highlighted a list of those resources that have helped me at the end of this book.

This is even more illustrated in Daniel 10. Daniel prayed to God for understanding but did not receive a response for almost 24 days. "Just then a hand touched me and lifted me, still trembling, to my hands and knees. And the man said to me, 'Daniel, you are very precious to God, so listen carefully to what I have to say to you. Stand up, for I have been sent to you.' When he said this to me, I stood up, still trembling. Then he said, 'Don't be afraid, Daniel. *Since the first day you began to pray* for understanding and to humble yourself before your God, *your request has been heard in heaven.* I have come in answer to your prayer. *But for twenty-one days the spirit prince of the kingdom of Persia blocked my way.* Then Michael, one of the archangels, came to help me... Now I am here to explain what will happen to your people in the future, for this vision concerns a time yet to come."[95]

Daniel's prayer had been answered from day one. But there was warfare in the heavenlies that prevented the answer from getting to him. However according to verse 2-3, he was in a place of targeted prayer and fasting.

"When this vision came to me, I, Daniel, had been in mourning for three whole weeks. All that time I had eaten no rich food. No meat or wine crossed my lips, and I used no fragrant lotions until those three weeks had passed." It was in that time that Archangel Michael was sent to release the answer to his prayers, so that he would no longer be hindered from understanding what God was trying to tell him.

We need to acknowledge the reality of spiritual warfare over our destiny and learn to pray effectively for victory.

God's Timing

As previously mentioned, God operates outside of our human understanding of time. His timing may not align with our expectations, and something we see as delayed may be perfectly on schedule, based on His divine plan.

In 2012 – during my 3 month cave season of solitude and prayer – I felt God had given me a detailed plan to do ministry on the streets of Toronto. He gave me direction from the daily schedule, the locations we were to serve at, and even the amount of money I should commit to pay each person who participated in the mission. God had been very specific, and I took Him at His word.

---

[95] Daniel 10:12-14

I reached out to quite a few people and invited them to serve with us full-time that summer. Serving involved helping the homeless, preaching the gospel and leading worship across the city. I knew that this mission was a labour of love, and for the amount of time they were going to put in, any amount I would give would be a small honorarium compared to the value of their time. I told them, "This is pretty much volunteering, but we will give an honorarium between $1,000 and $2,000 for the full summer to try and honour your time."

We left our homes around 10 am, and often returned home between 1-3 pm that summer doing the absolute most we could. We helped the homeless, brought food, played dominoes, ran Bible studies, led worship in churches, went to events, spoke, preached, and more. We saw God move and I was personally blown away seeing the Bible come to life that summer.

At the end of the summer we had a debrief session. There were so many testimonies about physical healings, salvation, deliverance etc. We were hyped reliving it all.

Then, one of my friends said, "Toyin, it was amazing what God did this summer. He made good on so many promises. However, there was one thing that did not happen." He paused.

"You told us we would receive an honorarium for our time, between $1,000 and $2,000. I'm not saying this because I came for that. If I wanted to make money this summer, I would have gotten a job. I'm bringing this forward because you said that God promised to provide those funds. Some of us do have responsibilities that we had planned to use that money for. So, what happened? Did you hear wrong, and God didn't say that, or He said it, but it didn't come through?"

I didn't have an answer. I said, "I honestly have no idea what happened. But what I do know is, God said it. I know He said it, because every other thing on that list of instructions He gave me about this summer happened. So, I know I didn't make it up."

I paused. We were all wondering the same thing. If He said it, and it didn't happen, then how could we explain the gap? We knew it was not because we had misspent the funds; we simply had never received enough for that. We barely had gas money for the van we used each day to travel across the city.

I said, "Maybe it's because I sinned. The truth is, I'm not perfect. I know I made mistakes this summer. Maybe that's it. Honestly, I don't have an answer, and I'm sorry." My friend asked, "Well, how are we going to receive the $2,000?" I admitted, "I have no idea. I'm going to try to work and make good on that commitment, but I don't know how long it will take." I was going to be returning to my part-time job, but that didn't cover my bills because I was still doing ministry work in the fall. I had no way to cover the $14,000 total I would need to pay everyone.

Admitting this to my team – who had worked so faithfully all summer long – was crushing. I had truly expected God to provide this money in a miraculous way, just like He had provided so many other miracles all summer long. But He didn't. Yet He never fails, so where did I miss it?

I remember praying at the Toronto House of Prayer a couple of weeks after that meeting. I tearfully asked God, "Abba, what happened? What did I miss? Why didn't the funds to pay the team come in?" There was no response.

I continued to journal and pray, "was it because of a mistake I made this summer?" I thought of my impatience, short-tempered moments or times when I held back from saying what He had told me to say out of cowardice etc.

Finally He spoke and said, "Toyin, I loved you enough to adopt you as my daughter when you hated me and actively sinned against me. So, why would I—now that you're my daughter—set you up for failure? If I loved you enough to bless you with the greatest of all gifts –salvation– why would you making mistakes, that you have repented from, stop me from blessing you?"

God continued, "Listen, if your perfection was the requirement for me to bless you as my daughter, then I would never bless you. You sin more than you know. You're remembering the few times you know you did something wrong this summer, but the truth is you sin almost every day. Yet, I take care of you and provide for you. I bless you. If you needed to be perfect before you could receive from me, then you would have failed before you started. So that is not the reason this didn't happen."

Wow. Okay. "Thank you Abba, so if it was not because I sinned, and I am your daughter, and you provide for me, then why didn't we see it come in?" I didn't get a response at all for the rest of that prayer time, and I moved on from the conversation. That was September 2012. By April of the next year, I had to decide whether we would do this summer ministry experience all over again.

I spoke to our leadership team and said, "I think Abba's telling us to do it again. But this time, I'm not promising any amount of money to anybody. Anyone that's participating will be doing it completely pro bono." I admitted, "But I'm so torn! I believe God is calling us to do this, but financially it makes no sense. At this point, my dad was having almost weekly conversations with me about where my life was going career-wise. They were expecting us to get normal jobs and do ministry in our off time.

We sat there thinking about what to do. At one point, I suggested working for The Salvation Army. That would tick both boxes; we'd be sharing the Gospel and getting paid consistently. But that wasn't what the Holy Spirit had put on my heart. It was the work of touring, ministering in song, preaching on the streets etc. We just didn't know what to do. One of our leaders, Mia Thomas said, "Okay everybody, let's pray in the Spirit until we know what to do."

After praying in the Spirit for a few hours, we felt our faith rising. All three of us came to the same conclusion: we were going to do the mission just the way He asked us to. Josh –fellow leader, now husband– said, "Jesus told us to do it in a specific format, let's do it His way. He will take care of us." We were fully bought in.

That was a Friday. On Saturday we posted an e-blast, announcing our plans to kick off with a seven-day prayer walk for the city on Monday of the next week. Then, on Sunday night, I got a call from a woman I've never met. She had just come back from a prayer retreat, and her friend had seen our e-blast. She told her about our prayer walk while on the bus ride home. She asked, "How can I support you guys?"

I said, "Well, you can join us for the prayer walk." She said, "Yes! I'm excited. I'm going to come and pray with you. But I want to support you in other ways. Can I give financially?" I thought about that. "Well... we have a van with a ton of issues. It's going to cost us around $1,500 to fix. Maybe you could donate $50 toward the van repairs?" She said, "Okay, thanks for letting me know. I'll pray about it. I'll let you know what I want to do."

On Monday she called again and asked, "Is there anything else you need?" I said, "Well, our main goal is to fix this van so you could maybe give a bit more toward that." I was moved that she was so open to giving us any amount toward the work.

On Tuesday morning she called again. "Hi, Toyin. The Lord said I should give you $37,000 for the work of your ministry." I was stunned. I responded, "I'm sorry what? I don't understand. We've never met before. You haven't even physically met me." She said, "I know, but I haven't been able to sleep the last few nights because I know this is what the Lord wants me to do. So, how quickly can I write you this check? I'm trying to get my sleep back!"

I was still shocked. We made plans to meet with the full leadership team, so she could get the full picture of our vision. Then she gave us a check for $37,000.

That $37,000 amount was exactly what we needed to give

everyone their honorariums from the previous summer, in addition to what we needed for the upcoming summer. It also covered the repairs to the van, and gas for the entire summer, which had been such a source of stress the previous year.

We called everyone from the 2012 summer meeting and let them know that God had provided miraculously. Each person received their honorariums of $1,000-$2,000. They were just as shocked as I had been. One of them said, what everyone was thinking - "Toyin, we know there is no chance you got this money through your part-time job. How did this happen?"

I said, "God is faithful to His Word. He showed up. He provided." And I shared with them how this woman had found us and sowed into the vision. I believe God received more glory in doing things this way, than if we had received those funds in the first summer.

The biggest lesson was that we saw the answer to God's promise *after* deciding to obey His direction, even after being crushed from the first year's disappointment. If we had decided to work with The Salvation Army instead of doing the summer program again, it would have been a similar work, but I would never have announced that 7 day prayer walk. She wouldn't have heard of our ministry. I don't know how many years it would have taken me to fulfill that promise my way versus God's way. The reason we saw the fulfillment of His promise was because we had a vision for obedience over the long term.

Testing and Maturity

At times, God will allow delays or what looks like

discrepancies in the fulfillment to test and refine your faith and character. One of the stories that illustrates this is the story of Lazarus in John 11:1-44. Please note the emphasis added as you read,

> Now a certain man was sick: Lazarus of Bethany, the village of Mary and her sister Martha... So [his] sisters sent word to [Jesus], saying, 'Lord, behold, *he whom You love is sick.*' But when Jesus heard this, He said, *'This sickness is not meant for death, but is for the glory of God, so that the Son of God may be glorified by it.'* (Now Jesus loved Martha and her sister, and Lazarus.) So when He heard that he was sick, *He then stayed two days longer* in the place where He was. Then after this He said to the disciples, 'Let's go to Judea again.'...
>
> He said to them, 'Our friend Lazarus has fallen asleep; but I am going so that I may awaken him from sleep.' The disciples then said to Him, 'Lord, if he has fallen asleep, he will come out of it.' Now Jesus had spoken of his death, but they thought that He was speaking about actual sleep. *So Jesus then said to them plainly, 'Lazarus died,* and I am glad for your sakes that I was not there, so that you may believe; but let's go to him.'...
>
> So when Jesus came, He found that he had already been in the tomb four days... So then Martha, when she heard that Jesus was coming, went to meet Him... Martha then said to Jesus, 'Lord, if You had been here, my brother would not have died. Even now I know that

whatever You ask of God, God will give You.' Jesus said to her, 'Your brother will rise from the dead.' Martha said to Him, 'I know that he will rise in the resurrection on the last day.' Jesus said to her, *'I am the resurrection and the life; the one who believes in Me will live, even if he dies, and everyone who lives and believes in Me will never die. Do you believe this?'* She said to Him, 'Yes, Lord; I have come to believe that You are the Christ, the Son of God, and He who comes into the world.'...

When Mary came to the place where Jesus was, she saw Him and fell at His feet, saying to Him, 'Lord, if You had been here, my brother would not have died.' Therefore when Jesus saw her weeping, and the Jews who came with her also weeping, He was deeply moved in spirit and was troubled... Jesus wept. So the Jews were saying, "See how He loved him!" But *some of them said, "Could this man, who opened the eyes of the man who was blind, not have also kept this man from dying?"*

So Jesus, again being deeply moved within, came to the tomb. Now it was a cave, and a stone was lying against it. Jesus said, 'Remove the stone.' Martha, the sister of the deceased, said to Him, 'Lord, by this time there will be a stench, for he has been dead four days.' Jesus said to her, 'Did I not say to you that if you believe, you will see the glory of God?' So they removed the stone.

And Jesus raised His eyes, and said, 'Father, I thank You that You have heard Me. But I knew that You always hear Me; nevertheless, because of the people standing around I said it, so that they may believe that You sent Me.' And when He had said these things, *He cried out with a loud voice, 'Lazarus, come out!'*

Out came the man who had died, bound hand and foot with wrappings, and his face was wrapped around with a cloth. Jesus said to them, 'Unbind him, and let him go.'"

Lazarus was not just anybody to Jesus; he was not a stranger. Twice in this passage we are reminded that Jesus *loved* Lazarus, and his sisters, Mary and Martha. Yet when he fell sick, Jesus does something confusing. Rather than go to Lazarus right away to heal him, Jesus intentionally stayed two more days in the place where He was. We know that Jesus was not only able to heal the sick but he had done it multiple times, without travelling to their location. It looked like Jesus was being very casual about somebody that He loved; He did not pray for Lazarus to be healed, or rush to his side.

When He decided to head over there, He knows Lazarus is already dead, but says, "He's just sleeping." He was so casual about it that His disciples really thought he was just asleep. Jesus had to clarify that he was in fact, dead. Because for God, raising Lazarus up from death was just as easy as waking him up from a nice, long sleep. This is how different God's perspective is from ours.

Jesus even said at one point, *this sickness is not unto death.* Yet he died. But God knew that that was not the end of the story.

When Jesus "finally" arrived at Lazarus' house, Martha and Mary were confused. They didn't understand why Jesus had delayed his coming. You can almost hear the pain and confusion in their words to him, "Jesus, if you would have just been here, my brother would still be alive." It's as if they're wondering, "Don't you care?" When Jesus sees Mary weeping and everyone else with her weeping, He groans in His Spirit and is troubled. He asks, "Where have you laid him?" They say, "Lord, come and see him," and then Jesus weeps.

I think about what would have caused Jesus to weep in that moment. He had seen hundreds of people sick and had healed many of them. He knew what He was about to do (raise him back to life). I wonder sometimes if He wept from seeing the people He loved in so much pain, when He was the solution they were looking for. Or maybe it was because they couldn't see what He was capable of.

Whatever it was, Jesus proceeded to call Lazarus out of the tomb, and the one who had been dead for four days, walks out. He is raised from the dead. Jesus has proven to be "the Christ, the Son of God." He shows He was true when He had earlier said, "this sickness is not unto death." And in doing things His way—not in the way that they expected—Jesus showed His power over death and fulfilled a prophecy that demonstrated that He is the Messiah.

Unlike others that Jesus had raised from the dead, the Jewish leaders tried to kill Lazarus and crowds would gather to see him. "When the large crowd of the Jews learned that Jesus was there, they came, not only on account of him but also to see Lazarus, whom he had raised from the dead. So the chief priests made plans to put Lazarus to death as well, because on account of him many of the Jews were going away and believing in Jesus."[96]

Why? The difference was that he was dead and buried for four days. As Johann Lange and Phillip Schaff explain in their commentary, it was important that Lazarus remained dead for four days before his resurrection. "Jewish mysticism teaches that a deceased person's spirit remains around the body for up to three days after death before departing. It was well-known in Israel 2,000 years ago that someone deceased could come back to life during this 3-day period but not afterwards.

On the fourth day, the spirit left the body and went to Sheol or Hades, and there was no hope for life without a miracle. Also, by the fourth day in Israel's hot climate, advanced decay would be destroying the body and the stench would have been overwhelming. When Jesus called Lazarus to life from the dead and healed his rotted corpse, the people knew that He was the true Messiah, performing genuine miracles as the prophets had foretold!"[97]

God will allow things to unfold differently, to help us see Him from a new perspective, to grow our faith and level of spiritual maturity.

This account emphasizes that our perspective is finite. God says through the prophet Isaiah, "His thoughts are not our thoughts, and His ways are not our ways. As far as the heaven is from the earth, that's how far His thoughts are from ours."[98] This is what encourages me when it feels like everything around me is falling apart. I can trust that there is

[96] John 12:9–11, ESV

[97] Lange, J. P., & Schaff, P. (2008). A commentary on the Holy Scriptures: John (p. 356). Bellingham, WA: Logos Bible Software.

[98] Isaiah 55:8-9

a perspective to this story that I just don't see, but eternally it will make sense.

When I look back on that most difficult political campaign, and the other difficult seasons of my life, they often make sense in hindsight. The only way you'll see the fullness of His purpose is by staying in this place of continual obedience. If you give into bitterness, discouragement or disappointment, if you let those emotions overwhelm you, they will cloud your outlook. They will stop you from stepping forward with Him.

Misinterpretation and Misapplication:

Sometimes, our misinterpretation or misapplication of what God said to us can lead to a misunderstanding about the meaning of what He said or the timing. The Bible says, "we know in part and prophesy in part,"[99] so the short answer is yes, you could have misinterpreted what the Lord said. We are human and whether we like it or not, our experiences and personal preferences can influence what we hear from the Lord.

One ditch I have seen people fall into is denying this, and assuming they hear the infallible word of God. Please don't fall into this type of pride. The only infallible word of God is the written word, the Bible. Everything else is coming through a filter. Yes, you can stand on the words You've heard from Him, but remember, we hear in part. Two things can be true at once. You can hear Abba lead you clearly in one sitting and misinterpret or misapply a portion of that message.

---

[99] 1 Corinthians 13:9-12

An example I shared earlier is when I thought the Lord told me who I was to marry. In hindsight, I realized that even though He spoke to me about many things, that specific "word" came from being in a sub-culture where a lot of women "heard from the Lord" who their husband was. Yet, God used even my mistake to draw my heart closer to Him in those two years.

Presumption

When God tells us A B C, we often assume the next step is D, E, F. What we don't see is maybe His actual plan is, A, B, C…G, D, T… pause… Z. U. B. (you get the point) Remember: our thoughts are not His thoughts, and our ways are not His ways. An example of this is when God told me to study for the MCATs. His specific directive was, "Study for the MCATs." As a human, I assumed that meant I was going to become a doctor.

I told a ton of people I was studying to be a doctor, when I went into my cave season (three months of solitude). And that's what God wanted: three months of my undistracted heart, fully present with Him. In those three months, He changed my life in multiple ways. I really thought I was going to be a doctor, but I felt Him invite me to a conversation about it before I started applying to med schools. When I finally asked him at the end of the 3 months if I was to apply to med schools, He said, "No."

I thought, "No? You told me to study for the MCATs. I've told everyone including my [Nigerian] father that I was pursuing medicine." He responded, "But I didn't tell you to apply to med schools, I didn't tell you to pursue medicine or be a doctor. I told you to study for the MCATs." Dang. He was right. Many times,

God gives us a directive and we extrapolate to make it mean different things. In actuality, he wants a specific result from a situation and lets us in on the plan step by step.

God used those 3 months to radically transform my life. That season triggered years of full-time ministry. It set me free to hear Him speak about my husband. It taught me to hear the voice of God for myself, instead of always depending on hearing through someone else. It changed my life and today, I am so grateful not to be a doctor after all. He knew what He knit me together[100] for, and the sight of blood while doing surgeries was not it!

God Knows What He's Doing…

Sometimes it's easy to get offended at God when we don't see Him come through in the way we expected. These situations create a beautiful opportunity for our hearts to stay pure before the Lord. We must be able to stay open, expectant, and receiving, even when we feel disappointed or confused. That's why it's so important to remember God knows what He's doing.

Even When It's Weird

Throughout Scripture, God speaks to His children and directs them in ways that would have felt—even for that period—uncomfortable. For example, John the Baptist was led by God into the wilderness, where he ate locusts and honey and was clothed in goat or camel hair. That was *weird*. Think about

---

[100] Psalm 139:13

this—God called John the Baptist to impact the multitudes and to spread a message of repentance, but He calls him to live out in the wilderness where nobody else is. How are you supposed to tell people to repent when you're sent to the wilderness where there are no people?

Yet, he owned the calling on his life, devoted himself to the message he had been given and the people came to find him. When Jesus talked about John the Baptist in Matthew, He said to people, "What did you go out to the wilderness to see?[101]" People were drawn to John the Baptist not just because he was obedient to the message God gave him, but also because of his consecrated life, as weird as it looked.

Even When It Defies Tradition

God can also call you to things that are completely out of your comfort zone. For example, when the Apostle Peter was leading the early church after Jesus had ascended back into heaven, he was used to centuries of Jewish tradition. He had been taught that Israel was the chosen people. Israel was the apple of God's eye. *They* were the people God had watched over throughout the ages. The Gospel of the Kingdom had been preached to Jews only, and people of other nations were considered to be outsiders. That was Peter's tradition.[102]

But then, Peter had a dream where God laid out in front of him a table of unclean animals. For all of Peter's life, he'd been taught it was not okay to eat these animals. Then God said, "Eat.

[101] Matthew 11:7-10

[102] Matthew 15:24

Do not call unclean what I have called clean." Peter didn't understand the dream. But as soon as he woke up, there were people in his home inviting him to visit Cornelius, a Gentile—an outsider—who had been visited by an angel. Because of the dream he just had, Peter agreed to share the Scripture with him and his household.

He didn't expect what would happen afterward. The passage says, "While Peter was still speaking these words, the Holy Spirit fell upon all those who were listening to the message. All the Jewish believers who came with Peter were amazed, because the gift of the Holy Spirit had also been poured out on the Gentiles. For they were hearing them speaking with tongues and exalting God. Then Peter responded, 'Surely no one can refuse the water for these to be baptized, who have received the Holy Spirit just as we did, can he?' And he ordered them to be baptized in the name of Jesus Christ. Then they asked him to stay on for a few days."[103]

Peter baptized these Gentile believers, even though it went against the years of tradition. Instead of refusing, he decided that if God decided to pour out His Spirit on all of them – especially after telling him in that dream, "Do not call unclean what I have called clean," – then they should be baptized. He responded in obedience to God's calling of the Gentiles, and today we are grafted into the family of God because of his and Paul's acts of obedience.[104]

---

[103] Acts 10:44-48
[104] Romans 11:11-31

QUESTIONS IN THE FIRE

Even At The Threat Of Death

When the church started to expand, persecution pushed the church into a mode of expansion. Stephen gets attacked for the Gospel message and becomes the first martyr. But before he is stoned to death, Stephen shares the Gospel message with his attackers, in love. Then—as they're stoning him—Stephen prays for them and says, "God, do not hold this against them."[105] Talk about obedience! Stephen may have felt like his work for God had just gotten started. He had just started to put himself out there sharing the Gospel. Then, it was done. How could God use his short-lived obedience?

The Bible says a man named Saul held the coats of the men stoning Stephen.[106] He was an accomplice in ending Stephen's life for sharing the Gospel. From Stephen's perspective, all he could probably see were people against the Gospel. But he didn't know that maybe there was a reason for Saul being there. Can you imagine the thoughts that went across Saul's mind while he watched Stephen *love* his attackers and pray for their forgiveness, while being stoned?

Yet Saul didn't change there. He continued going against the church and wanted to kill more believers and throw them in jail. However, he later encounters God, Jesus Christ. Then he gives his life to God, and he ends up doing the Gospel work; exactly what Stephen had begun. Saul, who is renamed Paul, also ends up writing most of the New Testament, which still guides believers today. Stephen couldn't have known it at the moment of his

---

[105] Acts 7:60

[106] Acts 7:58

death, but God used his final testimony to impact the Kingdom for thousands of generations.

Even When You're Persecuted

Sometimes we imagine that if we obey God, we'll be celebrated for it; but that may not be the case. Sometimes you can do exactly what God has called you to do, and be vilified for it. More and more, our generation defines good as evil and evil as good.[107] As a result, when you're willing to take a stand for God's way, instead of being celebrated, you can be persecuted.

In Acts 16:16-21, Paul prays for God to set a young slave woman free from demonic torment. She would follow Paul around Philippi as he taught people the Gospel. Her owners had used the demonic torment in her life as a source of profit. Paul recognized that she was worthy of being set free, and commanded the spirit tormenting her to leave.

You would think people would celebrate him for setting this woman free. After all, when Jesus healed the sick, people were happy. When Peter and John healed the lame man, people celebrated. When Paul healed other people, it was a good thing. But when he healed this woman, it triggered one of the biggest backlashes he experienced in his ministry. He ended up in jail for setting someone free from an oppressive spirit.

Here's what happens next. As Paul and his friend Silas are singing worship songs in their cell, an earthquake happens that breaks all their chains loose and opens the prison doors! Instead of escaping to preserve their lives, they convince all

---

[107] Isaiah 5:20

the prisoners to stay in the jail to save the life of the jailer. This act of selfless kindness leads to the jailer and his household to put their trust in Jesus. They're saved! Revival breaks out from Paul getting thrown in jail and worshiping God from his cell. The next morning, Paul is released from prison and keeps doing the work of the ministry.

God knew what He was doing when He prompted Paul to free the slave girl. He knew what He was doing when Paul and his companion got put in jail. He knew what He was doing when He sent the earthquake. None of it would have made sense to the people actually living it, but we see now that it led to multiple people coming to a saving knowledge of Jesus Christ.

Even When It Doesn't Make Sense

What do all these stories mean for us? It means we can have faith in God and practice moment by moment obedience, even when it doesn't make sense. Listen, God is *wise.* He knows what He's doing! He calls and directs us, "saying, 'This is the way, walk in it,' whenever you turn to the right or to the left."[108] He has a plan, and the closer we stick to Him, the more we get to see that plan unfold. His plan will be better than anything we could have come up with, more fun, more adventurous—and yes, sometimes it will be harder.

That's the experience of walking with God. If you say you want a history with God, then you get all of it. And out of the good, easy, hard, and painful, you get to experience multiple aspects of who God is.

---

[108] Isaiah 30:21

God's ways can be different from what you initially expected. If you could see everything that would come to pass when you first say *yes*, you would probably say *no*. By saying yes and following step by step, you are led into the abundant life He promises us. Yes, there are sacrifices that come when we obey, but there are also *amazing* treasures we receive when we trust God. I have received so many gifts because of radical obedience. There are moments where I thought I was doing something for God, and later realized, He wanted to do something for me. Some of the greatest treasures He's given me out of those moments of obedience have been two of my closest friends.

Gifts From Obedience

When I was working on my second album, I heard a woman sing at a church service. Her voice was amazing. I reached out and said, "Let's have a meeting. I want to share the heart of my album with you and see if we could work on this project together."

On the day we were supposed to meet up, she got lost. A trip that should have taken about an hour and a half, ended up taking her over three hours. I could tell by her text messages that she was getting increasingly upset and frustrated.

I was waiting for her in our student ministry office at York University and I thought to myself, "If she's mad, she's not going to be in a mental place to talk about my album and Jesus. I should just let her go back home and see if we can do this another time." I typed up a long message telling her that I could understand her frustration and it was okay to go home because it had already been a long day. Before I could press send, the Holy Spirit said, "*Delete that text message.*"

I didn't know why He said that. It felt obvious to me that I should just tell her to turn around. But, I deleted it. I sat patiently and kept on waiting. Finally she arrived after a 3 hour journey, still upset. Then we started to talk about the vision of the album. We ended up laughing and crying together. Today she is one of my best friends for over 10 years. She ran with me in ministry for close to six years, and has been one of my biggest cheerleaders. In fact, she met her husband through our ministry, and ended up getting married in our home because of the many journeys we have taken in the faithfulness of God. She has been one of the rocks that God gave to me as a gift. If I had told her to go back home that afternoon, I probably would have found somebody else in my local area. But by obeying God when He'd asked me to do this weird thing, He gave me the incredible gift of her friendship.

The second gift came in the York University library. As I was studying, someone sat beside me, and I felt the Lord ask me to share the Gospel with her. She was wearing a black "Christian" looking beret; don't ask me how a hat can look Christian, it just did. So, I did not share the Gospel with her. I thought, "Why would I share the Gospel with someone who's obviously dressed like a Christian? That would just be weird." I finished studying and left the library, but I felt the Holy Spirit repeat over and over, "I told you to share the gospel with her."

I felt so convicted that I turned around, went back up the stairs to the floor we were on. I found the cubicle where she was studying, and sat down beside her again. I knew it would look weird if I left, came back then started to speak. So I brought out my textbooks and pretended to study a little bit more all while thinking, "God, this doesn't make any sense." But I wanted to get it over with, so I turned around and blurted out, "Hi, my name's Toyin and I wanted to know if you know about Jesus Christ…" Before I could even finish my sentence, she said, "Oh my goodness, I'm a Christian too. I've been praying for God to please connect me to other Christians because I just moved here from Jamaica a couple of months ago. I didn't know where to start with meeting other believers…"

Wow. God knew she was a Christian and that she needed a godly community, and that this conversation would be the answer to her prayer. Today she is also one of my best friends and a rock in my journey. But if I hadn't spoken to her in that library, I probably would never have met her.

These two women are rocks for me. Our lives have become so intertwined, and we've been blessings to each other. But the reason we got connected in the first place was because of those moments of seemingly random acts of obedience that made no sense to me in the moment.

One of the reasons we often say things don't make sense, is because we want to save face. We want to be like everybody else. We don't want to feel uncomfortable or look different. We want to go along to get along. But something I've learned is that you need to be okay with looking different from the world when you are doing the things God calls you to do. If fitting in with the world is your goal, you will miss out on the abundant life God has for you.

God's Definition of Success

Finally, whenever you feel like you have fallen face first, I want you to remember that God's definition of success is different from what you see on TV and social media. When we think of "winning," we think about having wealth, a good family, a great career, winning elections, belonging to a large church, having influence, and so on. Other people would say, "I don't need anything extravagant—success is simply having comfort, peace, and being happy with myself."

But none of those ideas are God's eternal definition of success. Success does not mean getting the outcome you want. The definition of success is the process of complete obedience. Put differently, success is: To know God and be known by Him. To love God and be loved by Him.

I'm successful because whenever I have fallen face first, I got up and kept walking with the Maker of the Universe. I have a real, alive relationship with the Almighty God. The One who tore the veil so that we could come into the holiest of holies.

So success is your "yes" with action behind it. Even if everything inside is screaming NO. And because of that, I'm happy. Even when I had nothing in the bank account, I was happy. Even when I've lost elections I gave years of my life to, I've been happy. Even when people spat at me in the streets of Toronto because I was sharing the Gospel of Jesus Christ, I was successful: I knew I was exactly where He wanted me to be.

If you have obeyed God and felt like you fell flat on your face, let me be the first person to say congratulations. Your "Yes" was your win.

ACTIVATION POINTS

- Think about a time things didn't turn out as you expected despite believing you heard from God. What doubts or questions arose about whether you accurately discerned God's instructions? Bring those questions to Abba and allow Him to speak to you even if you don't fully understand.

- Consider a situation where people's decisions had an impact on your life. Forgive and release anyone that you have held responsible for affecting God's word over you. How can you continue to run in obedience despite other's decisions? How can you take ownership of your life of obedience?

- Review prophetic words you have received to see if they were conditional on certain actions or responses from you. Have you done your part? Can you do it now?

- Are there any patterns in your life, or family that need to be addressed with spiritual warfare prayers? Make a list of them and after reading chapter 10, take them to the Lord in prayer.

- Recall a situation where God's timing didn't align with

your expectations. How do you navigate the waiting period? Does it strengthen you or create doubt? What can you learn while you wait?

- Have there been any times when you misinterpreted or misapplied what you believed God said? If so, what caused you to believe what you believed? How can you guard against misinterpretation while staying open to Abba's guidance?

- How have you defined success thus far? How do you think God defines success? Where have you felt like you weren't successful even though you did what God told you to do? Take time to relinquish our human perspective and see that event from God's eternal perspective. What changes for you when you do that?

EITHER WAY YOU WIN

Chapter 10

HOLY SPIRIT - YOUR WILD CARD

And I will give you a new heart, and a new spirit I will put within you. And I will remove the heart of stone from your flesh and give you a heart of flesh. And I will put my Spirit within you, and cause you to walk in my statutes and be careful to obey my rules.
Ezekiel 36:26-27 (ESV)

My family and I are board game people. We love playing games together and one of our favourites is the Monopoly card game. In that game, there are wild cards you can use, which represent any property you need. Experienced players know that you want to hold the wild card until you have a stacked hand, then BAM! You slap the wild card on the table along with all your other cards. Even if it looked like you were the farthest from the endpoint, you can still win the game in that one move!

The wild card gives you a distinct advantage in the game because it can be anything you need it to be in order to win. Well, I have amazing news for you; the Holy Spirit is your wild card in the game of obedience. He is *everything* you need Him to be, at the moment you need it.

However, unlike receiving a wild card in a card game – which is often random and inconsistent – receiving the Holy Spirit is not a thing of chance. You don't have to shuffle the deck or cross your fingers hoping you get access. He is readily available to you. Unfortunately, most of us are completely sleeping on this knowledge! We are asleep to the power of the Holy Spirit! He is not only the One who calls us to obey, but He is the One who empowers us to follow through.

Too many people try to do what Jesus called them to do without leaning on the power of the Holy Spirit. That's like trying to compete in the Indy 500 with my first car, a raggedy rusted red 1988 Pontiac. It's a joke at best, a very frustrating experience at worst. You simply do not have the engine to do what God has called you to without activating His power that is available, and working inside of you.

There are certain assignments that God gives that require you to engage and activate the power of the Holy Spirit through prayer. Why? Because often when God gives you a mission to complete, the enemy does not watch you passively or cheer you on as you dismantle his kingdom, and release the kingdom of heaven on earth.

This book is an example of this.

The Prayer Breakthrough

In the Prelude, I talked about how stuck I was in the process of obedience with this book. The truth was I didn't know what was wrong and I didn't notice that I had delegated something God wanted me to do personally. I didn't know why something that was to take 6 months had taken over 2 years. I didn't know why I felt zero inspiration to complete the task, while doing so many other assignments He gave me during those 2 years.

It wasn't until I began to pray.

What do I mean? To be fair, I had never stopped "praying". I prayed almost everyday with my family and often alone. I even took 3-day solitude retreats; I went away every quarter to be alone with God, pray and seek His face. I even had a group of friends who were committed to praying on my behalf, and had done this for years, as we stepped into the different projects that God had called us to.

But I'm talking about a different type of prayer. You see, I was being specifically attacked in this area of obedience and I forgot that was even a possibility. One evening while I folded laundry–it seems God likes to speak to me while I do laundry–I was listening to a video with Tiphani Montgomery, a prophetess and international prayer leader. She was chatting casually with a friend of hers and said, "when I went viral, I knew that the enemy wasn't going to be happy about that. I didn't celebrate going viral. I immediately turned down my plate. Immediately." For context, "turned down her plate" means that she immediately went into a fast.

As soon as I heard her say she turned down her plate, I heard God say loudly to my heart, "Toyin, you are in a war and you are asleep. You think that the battles you are fighting are surface level. WAKE UP!"

He showed me how the enemy had been having a blast with my health, my husband's health, my finances, my business and I was doing nothing about it. We had so many different challenges coming at us from many sides in that season. One of them being a real estate court case on one of our properties. Every lawyer who reviewed the case said, "It's clear that this is a professional tenant scammer. This case being dragged out doesn't make sense. This should be a simple case in your favour." We had done everything we knew to do, but the situation felt like our hands were tied.

God asked me when was the last time I entered into an extended fast. This was to break off spiritual complacency, lean in to hear His voice, tap into His power, stop trying to do things in my own strength, and break off any chains that had been imposed on us.

I realized I had not entered into an intentional session of prayer *with* extended fasting for 5 years. With having children, I figured I couldn't do an extended fast while pregnant, or breastfeeding. I did have a gap year, but I had lost the discipline, and then got pregnant with my third child, and was now breastfeeding again.

In that moment, He showed me that my lack of discipline had also spread to my eating habits overall. I was eating a lot of sugar despite the immediate, negative impact on my body. I was praying for healing for my body while being undisciplined in my eating habits! What's more, I generally eat healthy foods, but in that season I was also snacking throughout the day.

I went from being undisciplined in one area, to it spreading throughout different areas of my life. I had eaten the fruit of comfort and complacency, and didn't notice it, even though it was killing me.

He said, "You're in a spiritual battle! And you're asleep! Wake up!" At that time, I thought he was just referring to the real estate challenge; as it had been stalled for almost a year.

At that moment, I decided to fast for a week for the first time in a long time. I 'turned down my plate' and He challenged me to pray in the Spirit for 30 minutes every day that week, in the middle of the day. I shared what I was sensing with friends, and some of them felt that that was a similar message for them; we began fasting and praying together. We didn't pray for anything specific, except for God to wake us up! We wanted him to break off the dross that had formed on our hearts, and stir up the fire of the Holy Spirit inside of us.[109] And God began to move.

He started to open our eyes to areas of compromise in our lives; places where we had given room to comfort and complacency without even noticing it.

Laying Down An Altar

At the end of the week, He invited me to continue the daily prayer at 12:30 pm EST, for a month. I was scared of saying yes. At this point, I pushed back and said, "Abba, how can I lead prayer every day, Monday to Saturday, in the middle of the day? That's the middle of the day! I'm often coaching, training my

---

[109] Matthew 3:11, Luke 3:16

team, or traveling." He responded, "Yes Toyin. You have gotten used to organizing time with Me in the place of prayer around your full schedule. Now you are going to organize your full schedule around prayer."

I thought, "But what if I can't be consistent? What if I fail at it? A month is a long commitment, I haven't done something like this in years–since I was in street and worship ministry."

"Toyin, are we really having this conversation?"

I realized that I was arguing with God about His invitation for me to pray. Wow! I knew immediately that my push back regarding this invitation–to extend the prayer for a month--showed that my time was not submitted to His leadership. I was trying to own my time while calling Him Lord.

I repented and informed those who were fasting and praying, that I would continue the times of daily prayer in the Spirit, and fasting once a week and not daily. Many of them shared that God has said the same thing to them as well; don't stop.

What happened next was crazy.

As we continued to meet over zoom every day for the next month, and the next, and the next, we started to see breakthroughs for each person. He started to sharpen our discernment and set us free from bondage to the fear of man. He set us free from social media addictions and living for people's opinions.

I saw specific areas where I started to make decisions in my business simply to please people, and He broke the bondage and manipulation off me. I came back so free and on fire, that team members and clients at different times said, "Toyin, you're back!"

I responded in true Toyin style, "I'M BACKKK BABYYYYYY!!!!" By the grace of God I could see where I had allowed people to manipulate my decisions and I was able to make decisions freely again. We lost the few clients I had spent months trying to please, who drained our emotions, time, and resources in one week of their own volition.

And as soon as they left, we had an influx of new clients who were our norm; they were grateful, and acknowledged what we were doing in their lives and businesses. People began to break through like they hadn't in months. It was truly as if a curse had been lifted once I stopped living to please and went back to walking in my gift. Over the next two months, we had our highest revenue months that year, back to back.

I could hear God's voice sharper, and clearer, than I had in years and was a better leader from that place.

At the time of writing this, we have been meeting everyday–except Sunday–to pray, for over six months. I never thought I could order my life around prayer in this way. I've missed a few meetings, but God isn't looking to throw down a hammer on us for "missing it". He is delighted by our weak yes! He is moved by our devotion and reach for more of Him.

What I didn't know was that, this season of fasting and prayer would open the door for breakthrough in a long list of battles. Our business broke through. My husband's hand was supernaturally healed. I was healed. I was able to discipline my eating habits again, and all the negative sugar symptoms left. God opened the door for me to meet Charlie Wetzel, John Maxwell's partner, and book writer (which I shared at the beginning of the book). Even more than meeting Charlie, I could sense God's leadership in this book writing process again. His fire and anointing came back. I had greater clarity and wisdom for how to do it, and you are now holding in your hands the fruit of that season of prayer.

You Need To Pray

As you step into a place of intensified obedience, you must recognize the need for prayer.

You need to pray for your marriage.

You need to pray for your children.

You need to pray for your career or business.

You must pray for your ministry.

You must pray.

There are things that will not change until you pray.

There are challenges that will not break until you pray.

You must pray. And if you don't already, you need to fast.

When Jesus came down from the mountain of transfiguration, He entered a situation where his disciples were attempting to cast out an oppressive spirit from a young boy. They had prayed for a long time and had not seen anything happen.

"Then Jesus rebuked the demon in the boy, and it left him. From that moment the boy was well."[110] The spirit left the boy *immediately*. His disciples were in shock. What were they missing? Why were they struggling and stuck in this place? Jesus came in and without struggle, and without force. In one sentence, this boy was completely healed and restored in his mind. Jesus explained that, "This kind does not go out except by prayer and fasting."[111] There are some matters that require prayer and fasting. Areas where your spiritual warfare will do more than your physical boldness, or smart strategies. You need to pray.

The Disciple's Prayer For Boldness

When Jesus left, He gave His disciples–including us–the great commission. They were obedient and went out to pray for the sick. When they healed the lame man at the gate called Beautiful, the High Priest called them and "severely [threatened] them, that from now on they speak to no man in [Jesus'] name."[112] Peter and John were bold in their response to Caiaphas, "Whether it is right in the sight of God to listen to you more than to God, you judge. For we cannot but speak the things which we have seen and heard."[113] But they didn't just speak with boldness and take that for granted. They went back to the company of believers and prayed!

"And being let go, they went to their own companions and

---

[110] Matthew 17:18 NLT

[111] Matthew 17:21

[112] Acts 4:16-18

[113] Acts 4:19-20

reported all that the chief priests and elders had said to them. So when they heard that, they raised their voice to God with one accord and said: "Lord, You are God, who made heaven and earth and the sea, and all that is in them... Now, Lord, look on their threats, and *grant to Your servants that with all boldness they may speak Your word, by stretching out Your hand to heal, and that signs and wonders may be done through the name of Your holy Servant Jesus.*"[114]

They could have said they were already operating in boldness, casting out demons, and healing the sick. They could have said they were already standing up to those who were trying to intimidate them and stop them from preaching the gospel. They could have said, "This is basic, we don't need to pray about it." Instead they asked with tenacity for boldness. They prayed so intensely that, "when they had prayed, the place where they were assembled together was shaken; and they were all filled with the Holy Spirit, and they spoke the word of God with boldness."[115]

If Jesus had to pray in order to walk with God on earth, you need to pray.

If Moses needed to pray in order to lead the people of Israel, you need to pray.

If Paul prayed continuously in order to spread the gospel. If he prayed despite being anointed enough to start multiple churches, and led revivals, who are we not to pray?[116]

---

[114] Acts 4:24-30

[115] Acts 4:31

[116] 1 Corinthians 14:18

The disciples did not try to fulfill the great commission from Jesus on their own, they prayed and asked for grace from God to accomplish the assignment. In fact, they "devoted themselves to prayer."[117]

We have gotten so comfortable, and so complacent that we forget that "we are not fighting against flesh-and-blood enemies, but against evil rulers and authorities of the unseen world, against mighty powers in this dark world, and against evil spirits in the heavenly places."[118] And you cannot fight a spiritual battle with earthly tactics; you fight in the place of prayer.

This book would never have been completed without God Himself. He revived my prayer life, and reminded me of the need to take this mountain in the place of prayer, before I could take it in my writing.

Many of us in North America talk about praying, but don't actually do it. We tend to say, "I'll be praying for you," and then move on. Maybe the prayers happen, but often they don't. You don't need to over-complicate the question of how to pray. You need the willingness to carve a little time out of your busy day and then, you just start talking. Talk to God like you would talk to an all wise dad and King who knows all, and loves you. It's that simple. Once you think about it that way, you can have any conversation you want with Him in the place of prayer.

---

[117] See Acts 1:14; 2:42; 6:4

[118] Ephesians 6:12

My Prayer For You

I pray that you would wake up from any area of complacency and bondage. I pray God would open your eyes to see areas where you have relinquished your authority. I pray that God would break up the hard areas of your heart and give you a heart of flesh. I pray for fire on your altar once again! I pray for a release of the power of the Holy Spirit in your life like you have never seen. I pray this in the mighty, and powerful name of Jesus. Amen!

ACTIVATION POINTS

- In what areas are you trying to figure things out on your own? What burdens or challenges is the Lord inviting you to release to Him?

- Consider areas in your life where you may have become complacent or comfortable. How might this complacency be hindering your obedience to God's calling?

- What does Jesus have to say about fasting and prayer in Mathew 6:5-18? Are they optional parts of the Christian faith or expected from us? Are they a part of your spiritual discipline?

- Read the following scriptures: Luke 3:21, Luke 5:16, Mark 1:35, Matt 14:23, Mark 6:46, John 6:15, Luke 6:12, Luke 9:18, Luke 9:29, Luke 11:1, Luke 22:32 - What can we learn from Jesus' example and prayer life?

- Are you willing to carve out dedicated time each day for

prayer, even if it means adjusting your schedule?

- Reflect on the Impact of Prayer: Think about times in your life when prayer has led to breakthroughs or transformations. How has prayer shaped your journey of faith?

- Take a moment to pray for renewal and empowerment in your prayer life. Ask God to awaken you from complacency, break any chains of bondage, and fill you afresh with the power of the Holy Spirit.

Chapter 11

PASSION. PURPOSE. WHAT BEING ALIVE FEELS LIKE

Lord, you alone are my inheritance, my cup of blessing.
You guard all that is mine.
The land you have given me is a pleasant land.
What a wonderful inheritance!
I will bless the Lord who guides me;
even at night my heart instructs me.
I know the Lord is always with me.
I will not be shaken, for He is right beside me.
Psalm 16:5-8

There is no higher joy than walking with the Most High God. No higher privilege than to be able to have a relationship with Him, hear His heart, follow His leadership, and reveal His grace and mercy to those around you.

While writing this book, myself and some friends had a

bible study session that completely blew my mind. We were studying the book of Mark, verse by verse, and had focused on Jesus' death and resurrection. In Mark 15:38 it said, "But Jesus let out a loud cry, and died. And the veil of the temple was torn in two from top to bottom." In that moment, God opened the door for us to have access to the Holy of Holies; this is incredible. Just imagine the odds of gaining access to a Holy God without this moment.

First of all, in order to experience the full presence of God, you needed to be within the Holy of Holies which according to Britannica was "the innermost and most sacred area of the ancient Temple of Jerusalem"[119], and was "accessible *only* to the Israelite high priest".

In order to do that, you had to be Israelite. Then you needed to be born into the tribe of the Levites, a direct descendant of Aaron. You then needed to be appointed or born into the right family line within your generational timeline as the High Priest. Even if you were chosen as the High Priest, you couldn't just go to the Holy of Holies anytime of the day or year because you wanted to connect with God. The High Priest went in once a year on Yom Kippur, the Day of Atonement, to burn incense and sprinkle sacrificial animal blood.[120] Oh, and I forgot to mention, you couldn't be a woman to do any of this.

Yet, the King of Glory opens the veil and allows you and I to, "Enter the holy place by the blood of Jesus, by a new and living way which He inaugurated for us through the veil, that is,

---

[119], [120] https://www.britannica.com/topic/Holy-of-Holies

[120]

through His flesh."[121]

Jesus' death and resurrection won us access to a Holy God. It won us access to forgiveness, and freedom from condemnation. We can enter boldly, freely, and this is what inspires our desire to obey Him! Since we have been given this open invitation, the least we can do is to give Him our lives in return. If we are going to represent Him in the world, then we need to die with Him at the cross, and accept the power, and life, that is also present in His resurrection. So what does being alive really feel like?

Abandonment to His Purpose For Your Life

If you want to build a history with God, then start with intentional, connected times of being in His presence. Read your Bible so that in the middle of all the distractions, you can hear His directions clearly. But don't just read for the sake of counting how many chapters you've completed; have a real conversation with Him. Bring your heart before Him. Ask God to show you His opinion of your decisions. Your life. Ask Him to show you His perspective. Ask Him what He is asking of you in this season.

Then when He speaks, take Him at His word. Pray bold prayers and trust Him with the outcome. Being alive is about stepping out on God's word and watching it come alive in front of you!

I remember the first time I read Mark 16:17 in this way. The first part says, "These miraculous signs will accompany those who believe: They will cast out demons in my name, and they will

---

[121] Hebrews 10:19

speak in new languages." Jesus spoke about casting out demons, and demonstrated it by freeing and healing those who came to Him. I saw more people than I could count get transformed after prayers of deliverance, and now understood why it was a large part of Jesus' and the disciples' ministry.

In Western culture, we tend to ignore the spiritual aspect of life. However, just because you choose to ignore the spiritual world, doesn't mean it does not have an effect on you. I have seen the repetition of generational curses and cycles like generational stagnancy, poverty, bitterness, divorce, etc. These things can be broken by the power of the blood of Jesus, through specific and targeted prayer. My dad is both a pastor, and someone who prayed for many people to be delivered from curses and oppression, so I knew the power of God is real. Still, in my heart, I figured it was for more mature believers, who had walked with God for decades.

One summer, we organized a prayer retreat for the volunteers in our ministry. We had the expectation that people would be set free from any level of oppression of the enemy. A lot of the people in that group had never been through a prayer for deliverance, and we were all excited.

Now, I had never led a prayer for deliverance myself before. Since we were meeting at the church my dad pastors, I scheduled that section of the retreat during my dad's office hours. I knew he would be in the building, so when the time came, my plan was to get him to come downstairs and pray for us. While I didn't tell my dad any of this, I knew he would be willing. He loves to pray.

Things were going exactly according to schedule. While I

taught on the biblical foundation for deliverance, my dad came into the church for office hours. He popped his head in the sanctuary doors, said, "Hi everyone!" and went upstairs to his office.

Perfect. I continued teaching for about 30 minutes, then wrapped up my teaching. Once done I announced, "Now that we have learned the theology behind the importance of praying for and expecting deliverance in Jesus' name, it's time to put it into practice. Give me a second. I'll be right back." I ran upstairs to get my dad to come and pray deliverance for all of us.

Except his office was empty. There was no one there.

I checked all the rooms, the offices, the washroom, everything. He was gone. I didn't have my phone with me because we all put our phones away for the retreat. I ran outside to find his car; not there. I realized he was gone. He had left early that day, probably to give us space.

"What now?" I stood outside the church building with everyone inside waiting for me. I thought to myself, "Toyin, you just told these people that Jesus is about to set them free from oppression. You told them the Bible is real, alive, and that God can do this through any of us. You said this is not just for special Christians, and there's no such thing as superhero Christians."

I felt the Lord say, "Go back in and get it done."

"Okay. Got it," I responded. Cue heart pounding, sweat glands activated, and praying under my breath. I didn't try to do anything extravagant. I called out Bible verses, and gave prayer directives. Thankfully, I had one of my dad's workbooks with specific scriptures to pray for multiple different issues, as well as another workbook from another deliverance teacher I had learned from. We prayed simply, and God showed up.

By the end of that day, people had been set free from all sorts of oppression. Some people had been physically healed, and I knew without a shadow of a doubt that it was not because I made it happen. *It was Jesus, honouring His own word.*

That retreat happened around ten years ago. Since then, I've led a number of other "Freedom Sessions." In these ten years, people have been healed from schizophrenia, daily migraines, masturbation, pride, and deep fear, to name a few. In one of the initial prayer meetings, a sister in Christ had been dealing with life-threatening asthma all of her life. As we were praying for her, she had an asthma attack. I prayed, "God give wisdom and heal her now!" From that prayer session she was completely healed and delivered from asthma. Years have passed and she's confirmed that she has remained healed.

Another sister who woke with headaches every day, for almost ten years, participated in a Freedom Session. For the first couple of days afterward, she messaged us each day to let us know she woke up with no headache. She added, "Don't worry. I'm not going to message you every day for the rest of my life, but do you understand how freeing it is to wake up without a headache after years of waking up with one every morning?"

My point is that we aren't special people. This wasn't a large evangelistic meeting. It was simply getting together, praying, and expecting God to show up.

I know without a doubt that my seasons of shutting out the noise, seeking Him in solitude, and personal prayer retreats, is a large part of what helped me develop an ear for the voice of the Lord. Not only that but they helped develop the freedom to step out and trust Him in these random adventures.

Joy-filled Surrender

When I was in my ministry season, my friends and I made a lot of sacrifices to do what God called us to do. In the beginning of our time working together, there was a point of indirect competition. It felt like we were wrestling for the "suffering" trophy. We would talk about who's giving up the most or who's sacrificed the most. We would talk about it in a boastful way. We'd say things like, "I couldn't do [that], and [this] is what I'm laying down for Him." We were so focused on what we were giving up for Christ that we stopped being thankful. We were complaining and grumbling all the time, which impacted our joy.

One day, Abba said, "Toyin, I've done much more than you. I died on a cross and carried the sin of the world. It doesn't matter what sacrifice you make. It doesn't compare to what I have done." He led me to Malachi 3. I was used to reading this chapter because it talks about not keeping our tithes and offerings from the Lord. But this time, verse 8 stood out, "Would anyone rob God? Yet you are robbing Me! But you say, 'How have we robbed You?' In tithes and offerings."

I was confused. "Abba," I responded, "I am paying my tithes and offerings." In fact, I thought it further justified the "sacrifices" I was making for the sake of following Him. He told me to keep reading, and there it was, in verse 13-15, "Your words have been arrogant against me, says the Lord." I paused. It continues, "Yet, you say, "What have we spoken against You?" I thought, "I don't speak against you Abba, I'm doing all this for you. What do you mean?"

Verse 14 says, "You have said, "It is pointless to serve God; and what benefit is it for us that we have done what He required, and that we have walked in mourning before the Lord of armies?" So now we call the arrogant blessed and those who do wickedness are built up, but they also put God to the test and escape punishment..." He was speaking directly to my heart. God was saying, you're doing what I called you to do, but you're making me out to be wrong with all your complaints.

I began to pray and repent, and called a friend of mine to show her what He had said to me. When I called, she said God had just spoken to her from Malachi too! The verse she was led to was Malachi 1:13, "You say it is too hard to serve the Lord. You've turned up your noses at my commands. You're offering me lame sacrifices." Both of us fell on our faces in repentance.

Sometimes we obey God with a grumbling heart. It's like dragging a child along on a beautiful hike. They can't see the scenery, the beauty, and the joy of the moment because they focus on the difficulty of the walk.

In Exodus, the Israelites complained nonstop after God freed them from Egypt and guided them toward the promised land. And because of their grumbling, they never received the promise.[122] My friend and I were grateful that God pointed out our sin of grumbling, complaining, and making it about us. It was the mercy of God to check our hearts in this way.

Watch that you aren't exalting your sacrifices above what Jesus has already done for all of us. This shift in focus will help you stay in a place of joy[123] and gratitude while serving, instead of negativity and complaining.

It is an honour to walk with a living God. There is no sacrifice that God can invite you to make that is greater than the sacrifice He made on the cross. In crushing His own Son so that we could be forgiven, Jesus paid the ultimate sacrifice. That reminder often helps me to keep things in perspective. We are not the Messiah, He is.

When we "set [our] minds on the things that are above, not on the things that are on earth,"[124] we are released from the competitiveness, the pettiness, the opinions of others, and anything that easily weighs us down and distracts us. When we are freely given to the will of God in our lives, we stop caring about what others think. We simply live. We simply go– and it is such a freeing place to be– unbothered and unshackled with the cares of this world.

This is not about personality, it's about being personally connected to the One who fuels our lives. I have seen friends with radically different personalities also take these exciting missions from the Lord in different arenas and see the hand of

---

[122] Numbers 14:26-38

[123] See Psalm 119:2 and Psalm 37:4.

[124] Colossians 3:2-4

God show up in radical ways that ignite joy and hope in their hearts! Here's the thing, God is waiting for you to step up so He can back you up! God reminded Asa when he turned away from Him that, "The eyes of the LORD search the whole earth in order to strengthen those whose hearts are fully committed to him."[125]

When we commit our hearts to Him, He strengthens us, whether that is in your parenting, job, business, exercise, mentorship, or relationships. God wants to show off with your life, for His name's sake. So that when people see what He does with your surrendered life, they say, "This can only be God." Your life is for His glory and His fame, And it is an incredible way to live.

A Consecrated Life

Part of the joy of walking with the Lord is the beauty He has in the place of holiness. When God calls us to live differently from the world, it honors our Holy God, and it also blesses us tremendously. The Holy Spirit isn't called "holy" by mistake. It is intentional and a core part of who God is. He is completely separate from any thing or person we can imagine.

We must follow His leadership in areas of morality *if* we are His disciples.

If you come to the end your life with tremendous stories of walking with God, but you were abusing the people in your home, cheating in business ventures, breaking commitments etc., you've missed the entire point.

[125] 2 Chron 16:9

The Bible says, "do not be conformed to this world, but be transformed by the renewing of your mind, so that you may prove what the will of God is, that which is good and acceptable and perfect."[126] If you are asking God to let you know His will for your life in this area, there are a few things He has made abundantly clear that He desires from us!

Fight For Sexual Purity

As a culture, we have gotten comfortable and casual with sexual immorality. We have entire websites dedicated to married people interested in affairs, have normalized people living together, and casually having sex outside of marriage. It breaks the heart of God. As a culture, we have stopped highlighting God's standard because we fear the repercussions from people.

First Thessalonians 4: 3-4 says, "For this is the will of God, your sanctification; that is, that you abstain from sexual immorality; that each of you know how to possess his own vessel in sanctification and honor..." God cares about your sexual purity.

So just in case you need this reminder, "Flee sexual immorality. Every other sin that a person commits is outside the body, but the sexually immoral person sins against his own body. Or do you not know that your body is a temple of the Holy Spirit within you, whom you have from God, and that you are not your own? For you have been bought for a price: therefore glorify God in your body."[127]

Back when Josh and I were courting, I broke a commitment

---

[126] Romans 12:2

[127] 1 Corinthians 6:18-20

I made to the Lord about kissing Josh before we were married. When I came to Him to repent, I said, "Abba, I was overcome with–" He interrupted me, and brought to mind the scripture that says, "No temptation has overtaken you except something common to mankind; and God is faithful, so He will not allow you to be tempted beyond what you are able, but with the temptation will provide the way of escape also, so that you will be able to endure it."[128]

Then He pointed me to Romans 6, which reminded me that "our old self was crucified with Him, in order that our body of sin might be done away with, so that we would no longer be slaves to sin; for the one who has died is freed from sin."[129]

He then challenged me with this, "Therefore sin is not to reign in your mortal body so that you obey its lusts, and *do not go on presenting the parts of your body to sin as instruments of unrighteousness*; but present yourselves to God as those who are alive from the dead, and your body's parts as instruments of righteousness for God. *For sin shall not be master over you,* for you are not under the Law but under grace.[130]

He said to me, "Toyin, you weren't overcome with sin. You chose it. Own it. Repent for it. And don't choose it again. Don't present your body to sin as an instrument of unrighteousness. Don't be alone with Josh in contexts that will allow you to cross the line. Simple." Dang. There is no sugar-coating things with Abba because He knows our hearts. He died for our freedom

---

[128] 1 Corinthians 10:13

[129] Romans 6:6-7

[130] Romans 6:12-14

from sin. For us to say "we were forced to do it" minimizes His work on the cross.

So what did Josh and I do? We called our ministry friends and let them know that we could not be the last two people in the bus at drop-off time (drop-offs often ended at night). They helped us in this area the rest of that summer. We rearranged the drop off schedule, and the few times we were the last two in the van, they would call us and stay with us on speakerphone until one of us got home, to keep us accountable.

Fight For Holiness

Fight for your holiness! Don't listen to the people around you who want to minimize sin in any capacity. When the Holy Spirit convicts you of sin even if it is something that isn't a "big deal" to those around you, run away. We cannot delight in our sin instead of being broken about it and call ourselves friends of God.

God also cares about how we live in general. He is not removed from our everyday habits. While it's easy to highlight sexual immorality as an area to be obedient, I believe we can forget the overall call to live in a consecrated way.

The Bible says, "We urge you, brothers and sisters, admonish the unruly, encourage the fainthearted, help the weak, be patient with everyone. See that no one repays another with evil for evil, but always seek what is good for one another and for all people. Rejoice always, pray without ceasing, in everything give thanks; *for this is the will of God for you* in Christ Jesus"[131]

---

[131] 1 Thessalonians 5:14-18

I've heard people call themselves cussing Christians, and some believers and leaders in the Body of Christ use foul language both in secret and on platforms. Yet the word of God says, "Don't use foul or abusive language. Let everything you say be good and helpful, so that your words will be an encouragement to those who hear them."[132]

Please hear me, being adopted into God's kingdom changes us. If you are not being changed into more of the image of God, if you are not being convicted about laughing at, and sharing coarse jokes and foul stories, if you are completely comfortable in drunkenness and sexual immorality– and you are saved–you need to ask the Lord to revive your heart! God's Spirit is called Holy before it is called anything else. And while the Holy Spirit *will* inhabit a broken sinner, He will *not* leave you as is, comfortable in our mess. He will convict and transform you.

A song I released called "Revive My Heart" speaks to this - He will be treated as Holy by those who will enter His glory!

For the Lord gives wisdom;
From His mouth come knowledge and understanding.
He stores up sound wisdom for the upright;
He is a shield to those who walk in integrity,
Guarding the paths of justice,
And He watches over the way of His godly ones.
Then you will discern righteousness, justice,
And integrity, and every good path.
For wisdom will enter your heart,

---

[132] Ephesians 4:29

And knowledge will be delightful to your soul;
Discretion will watch over you,
Understanding will guard you,
To rescue you from the way of evil,
From a person who speaks perverse things;
From those who leave the paths of uprightness
To walk in the ways of darkness;
Who delight in doing evil
And rejoice in the perversity of evil;
Whose paths are crooked,
And who are devious in their ways;
To rescue you from the strange woman,
From the foreign woman who flatters with her words,
Who leaves the companion of her youth
And forgets the covenant of her God;
For her house sinks down to death,
And her tracks lead to the dead;
None who go to her return,
Nor do they reach the paths of life.
So you will walk in the way of good people
And keep to the paths of the righteous.
For the upright will live in the land,
And the blameless will remain in it;
But the wicked will be eliminated from the land,
And the treacherous will be torn away from it.
Proverbs 2:6-22

I love how Brendan Witton, lead Pastor of Toronto City

Church outlined how to break off the bondage of sin from your life:

1. Don't give sin more power than it has. You are already free in Christ.
2. Reach the point of no return and make a decision to cut that sin out of your life.
3. Don't call it something different from what it is. If it's sin, call it sin, and turn away from it.
4. Repent. Confess to God, confess to a mature spiritual friend or mentor, and realign yourself with God's will to remove these obstacles.

God is not Santa. Any voice that consoles you to stay in your sin is not His voice! He is still holy.

Forgiveness

Obedience looks like being willing to forgive. We can't pursue the will of God while carrying offenses toward people, situations, and institutions. On this topic, I would recommend reading *The Bait of Satan: Living Free From the Deadly Trap of Offense,* a book by John Bevere. I read this once a year, every year. If there are any situations where I'm still harboring offense, I get to acknowledge and process it with the Lord. A song that I would highly recommend after reading that book is "A Heart that Forgives" by Kevin Levar.

Community

It takes community and accountability to obey God over the long term. Jesus called the disciples to Him individually, but then He had them run together. Even when He sent them out to minister and bring healing to others, He sent them out in twos.

As wise and as effective for the gospel as the Apostle Paul was, he also had Godly friends around him, and listened to them when it was needed. In his letters, he often identifies them by name. Many times it's Paul and Silas, Paul and Barnabas, or Paul and Mark; community saved Paul's life, more than once. In Acts 19:25-41, when people were trying to kill Paul in a riot, he felt bold and wanted to face the crowd. His community told him to sit this fight out and he listened. He stayed out of view and the riot ended. At another time they told him not to go to Jerusalem, but this time he went, knowing they were speaking from fear.[133] And Paul, in turn, kept Peter accountable when he behaved in a hypocritical way.

In Acts chapters 2, 4, and 6, we see a community that knew each other's needs and supported one another. We go through much unnecessary hardship because we are often unwilling to ask for help. We don't lean on our God-given community.

I used to resist asking for help for many years. I believed that I could ask God directly, but not people. I would point to scriptures like, "I lift up my eyes to the hills from whence He cometh. My help comes from the Lord, the maker of heaven and Earth,"[134] to imply that God does not send us help in the form of others. I didn't want

---

[133] Acts 21

[134] Psalm 121

to ask for help from other people. My mentality was, "God can speak to the people, and the people will help."

While Nehemiah served in King Artaxerxes' court, he got news about the destruction of Jerusalem's walls. He couldn't keep from looking visibly disturbed, and the king asked him why he was sorrowful. He shared the reason and the king asked him, "What do you request?"

Here's what Nehemiah did not do. He did not leave the palace, find his prayer shawl, a quiet corner, and pray for God to communicate his need to the king supernaturally. The Bible says he, "prayed to the God of heaven," and then "said to the king…"[135] He verbalized his request directly to the person most able to help him make a difference.

You need community. You cannot do this on your own. However, it takes humility to be willing to admit that.

Community can also protect you from making unnecessary mistakes. When we stay humble enough, and remain connected with other people, we allow them to see our lives. Being willing to have real transparent relationships, means that when you make mistakes, you can bring it to the table without judgment, and be restored every time. People who miss this start off on fire and after a few years of going at it alone often find themselves far from the truth they once knew.

I have shared multiple instances where I would have gone sideways had it not been for intentionally steeping myself in community, with active accountability. I keep an open door, and open heart to hear my friends, leaders, and even those I lead,

135 Nehemiah 2:4, 5

PASSION. PURPOSE. WHAT BEING ALIVE FEELS LIKE

speak to my character. I would rather have the conversation with people and God here on this side of eternity, than find out the glaring flaws that hindered my witness of God's love, grace and mercy after I leave this earth.

Accessing the Supernatural

Many people are focused on convincing the masses about the Kingdom of Heaven with a lot of preaching and talk, yet we are often just as tired, bored, distracted with entertainment as they are. People want proof. They want to see if this is real. This was also true of Jesus's generation. That's why, everywhere Jesus went, He did good, healing the sick, and setting free all who were oppressed by the devil.[136] He demonstrated the power of God and it was undeniable.

Living in the supernatural means being open to the power of God flowing through you in every context. Whether in the marketplace, ministry, family, with your friends, shopping, or at a funeral, Holy Spirit wants you to be a vessel that He can speak, heal, share words of knowledge, and words of wisdom through. That is what living in the supernatural looks like.

You don't need to speak in "Christianese" in order for Jesus to use you. You can be excellent at what you do, and pray for that person who needs it in your office. That prayer doesn't need to be five minutes long with your eyes closed, rocking and praying in other tongues in order to be effective. It can simply be, "Abba please heal this headache in Jesus name," and that's it. When Jesus does it, they know your God came through for

---

[136] Acts 10:38

them. God's power can work through you in simple, natural, authentic ways.

People experience God's power in different ways through the gifts of the Holy Spirit. Sometimes, you'll pray, and God's gives you the wisdom they need for that situation. At other times, there might be instant, supernatural, physical healing. The Holy Spirit will flow however He is most needed. You can also operate in different gifts depending on the season.

There was a technical challenge in our business that had been bugging us for a couple of years. I finally prayed, "Abba, we need wisdom. I don't know how to go around this." That night, I had a dream. In the dream, I was sitting down with our then-director of operations and she said, "You know, this thing? All we have to do is…" And she went ahead to explain, step by step, how we could fix the problem. I woke up, called her immediately, we implemented it, and it worked!

So how do you access this power? First, understand it's always available to you. All you have to do is ask. Scripture says, if you ask, you'll receive. If you seek, you will find. If you knock, the door will be opened to you.

Remember, as God moves you further along in the journey of obedience, each level will require more than you can do in your own power. This allows you to stay in a posture of trust and dependence, and that opens the door for God to bypass protocol and do what only He can do.

Read

The more you read the Bible, the more clarity and direction

you'll experience in your prayers. Sometimes we may pray for something that Scripture actually forbids, when we are not familiar with the Bible.

Imagine if someone spent their life robbing banks, and then got saved. That person might pray, "God, could you please help me to be successful in my next robbery?" Based on what we know of God's heart from the Bible, God won't answer that prayer! Until that person recognizes God's Word, "You shall not steal," they won't know what prayers He's likely to answer or not. If you really want to grow in prayer and fall more in love with God, you need to read His Word.

The Bible will also give you examples of how to pray, where to start, and how to do it. For example, John 14:15 says, "If you love Me, you will keep My commandments." That Scripture has taught me to pray a similar idea to Abba: "I ask that you help me to truly love you with everything inside of me. God, I pray that you would give me the grace to obey you, to keep your commandments, to do what you're asking me to do. I feel tired right now. I know I'm doing everything you've said, but I need your grace to stay here and continue to obey. So, could you help me?" I will pray my way through other verses in the same way.

Scripture also shows us multiple examples of people who took action after praying. In 2 Chronicles 20:1-30, Jehoshaphat took time to pray and seek God's direction and help when the Moabites and Ammonites (enemies of Israel) came against him. He then implemented the direct and specific guidance God had given him in that place of prayer. In this case, they "began to sing and to praise" and their enemies "helped to destroy one another." Acting on God's word, after you've prayed is a key step in building a history with God.

Choose Courage

Courage is saying yes to what God calls you to do. Many people are very comfortable with all the don'ts: don't watch that, don't go there, don't talk to that person, don't listen, don't laugh. But courage is also saying yes. It's choosing to do what He says to do, even and especially in the small areas of obedience that nobody else will ever see. If you don't learn how to say yes in the hidden place, you will not have the muscle capacity or ability to say yes to God in the public place.

Many people look at the lives of successful people and assume it just happened. For instance, a person might say, "Tiger Woods won his first open when he was 21, an overnight success!" But the truth is, Tiger Woods first picked up a golf club at the age of 18 months. It's the muscles you build in private that determine your choices in public. It's also the compromises we make in private that often hinder us in public as well.

Courage looks like saying yes to God even when your pride gets in the way. Courage looks like saying yes, even when you could get away with saying no.

It takes courage to act. To move forward in the things God has given you to do. But without action, what happens to our prayer? What if Jesus had stopped at prayer, and never took action? In the garden of Gethsemane, He prayed so fervently that

His sweat fell to the ground like drops of blood.[137] Imagine that he followed that up by saying, "Well, that was a great prayer meeting. Did you see that sweat? I prayed like nobody has ever prayed before." And then went home to eat some fish and bread.

No! He followed that prayer with action. He walked to the cross, endured all the way to death and then rose again. Because of His *action*, we are saved. If Jesus had stopped at prayer, none of us would be saved right now. Our Master and highest example was a man of prayer, but also a man of action, even unto death.

Jesus said, "You don't take my life. I lay my life down."[138] He had the power to call legions of angels to stop the whole drama. At any point, on the way to the cross, He could've decided, "I don't want to do this anymore." But He was committed to see His Father's will through, unto death. He says in prayer, "Father, if You are willing, remove this cup from Me; yet not My will, but Yours be done."[139] And again He says, "My food is to do the will of Him who sent Me, and to accomplish His work."[140]

Doing the will of God and accomplishing His work; this is life. This is what God asks of us. Jesus didn't say, "My food is to pray and be in the presence of God." He said, "My food is to act and do the thing God is calling me to do." That includes prayer, it includes being alone with God, but it also includes taking action. Jesus asks for the same follow through from us. At the end of John's gospel, after His resurrection Jesus speaks with Peter; this was after Peter's denial on the morning of Jesus'

[137] Luke 22:44
[138] John 10:18
[139] Luke 22:42
[140] John 4:34

crucifixion. He asks Peter, repeatedly, "Simon, son of John, do you love Me?" The Scripture says, "Peter was hurt because Jesus asked him this three times. After the third time Peter answered, 'Lord, you know all things; You know that I love You.' Jesus said to him, 'Tend My sheep.'"

Jesus didn't say, "Do you love me? Well, let's have a nice prayer meeting, and a good worship service. Or—better yet—how about we just talk about it?" He was very specific with Peter. He said, "Here's what loving me looks like for you, Peter. You are in charge of the church right now. Feed my sheep."[141] If He was that specific with Peter, then why would He not be willing to direct us in the same way? We are called to be people of action: people who pray, listen well, and then act.

It's not uncommon to hear someone pray for the nations at church. They might say something like, "Lord, help our leaders. Heal our nation. Bring peace. Help people to come to a saving knowledge of Jesus Christ." It's less common for us to act in small ways to bring healing to the big areas we pray about. If you're going to pray for your nation, consider whether you are taking care of your neighbor. Have you said hi? Do you know their names and are you intentional about building relationship with them?

God wants you to work with Him to be the answer to your prayers. When we ask for His help, so often what He gives us – if we're willing to listen – is a plan for how we can be instruments of help in the areas we're praying about. Remember, God's love language is obedience. He says, "Look, if you say you love me and

---

[141] John 21:15-17, paraphrased

I am a priority to you, then you will do what I ask you to do."[142] For many of us, it's easy to live however we want. It's easy to do a couple of external things to show love for God like singing, reading the Bible, prayer, and other religious activities, and then we call it a day. But those fall short of what He's actually asking of us. Singing songs, reading the Bible, going to church meetings – all those things are great – but alone, these things are not the culmination of your worship. Worship is a lifestyle.

Rest

Many of us have an achievement mindset that does not allow room for rest and rejuvenation. Without rest, you are more likely to ignore the small details that would maximize your time and energy. When we ignore the importance of rest, we fall into traps set by the enemy for our emotions or break down physically. Rest is important for longevity of whatever message or task God has given you. Even God rested on the 7th day of creation.[143]

Some say, "I would rather burn out than rust out." But it doesn't have to be either/or. It doesn't have to be that you are a blazing spark for three years, non-stop, and then you're burned out, or that you've turned away from your love for God.

When I was younger, I did not care about rest. I was driven to do what God was calling me to do, non-stop. I would only rest when I got sick. Then I'd be in bed for three days to a week.

Then I'd recover and keep going. I used to be proud that I

---

[142] John 15:14, paraphrased

[143] Genesis 2:2-3

could function on four hours of sleep every day, but rest and Sabbath is a sign that we are willing to do our part, and allow God to do His. To trust Him with the outcome. You are not His workhorse. You're His daughter or son.

It took years for that message to get through, eventually it began to sink in. I realized that rest is a function of trust. God asked, "Can you let go and trust that I will keep this thing going without your help? Can you trust that it depends on Me, not on you?" For me, the first step was as simple as getting eight hours of sleep a day. It sounds so basic, but at first, I felt guilty to get that much sleep. I thought I was being lazy.

What I realize now is that I get more done during my waking hours if I've slept about six to eight hours, than if I sleep for four hours and I'm groggy or sleepy throughout the day. Prioritizing rest can help you be more creative, intentional, make less mistakes and happier overall. My character is better. A few things I thought were character issues, were a direct result of sleep deprivation. You may think you have an overeating issue, or an anger issue when really you just need to get some sleep.

With the neuroscience coaching we do, I often see situations where someone is not operating at their best because of a lack of rest (not just physical sleep, but a tired brain). You will often find me brainstorming ways for clients to get deep rest–to rejuvenate their bodies and brains–so that they can function at their absolute best. God cares about your health and your body's wellbeing, but many people are operating in a fight or flight state. You may think those things don't matter–and keep pushing yourself–but eventually it will burn you out. Take it from me, rest. Pause, so that you can keep going forward in the most optimal state. God is so serious about rest that it is a command.

Sabbath

Sabbath is a big part of my life and walk with God. It's also been a huge contributor to my increased productivity in obeying him. Sabbath is when we take time weekly to stop our work, and rejuvenate personally, with friends or family. It's to spend some time with Him and make sure you aren't going non-stop week after week. Specifically, He says we are to keep the Sabbath "holy" separate and focused on Him. It can also look different in different seasons. In fact, the day of the week that I take my "Sabbath" rest often varies depending on when I was working. When I was in Ministry, and worked on the weekends, I took Thursdays off. In another season, I took Mondays off.

You may not be able to get a two-day weekend every week, but often, even when we do, we fill that time with so much activity we aren't truly getting a break. For instance, If you have young children, they will follow your cue for what is expected on days off. In our family, we enjoy "couch" time, play a few board games, laugh together, but there doesn't have to be a high energy output. Make the decisions that serve you, your family, and that help you to focus on what matters most.

You must take responsibility for your own rest. Plan a sabbath. Ideally, each person in your family should have their day to rest. Whether or not you can coordinate those sabbath times to overlap, you'll still come back to your loved ones feeling refreshed. Enjoy the moments of coming together as a family. Chill. Seek the Lord together. Be with one another.

Out of solitude, rest, and sabbath, God ushers us into community. And because of how He's refreshed us and spoken to us during those times of personal worship, we are able to be fully present, with wisdom and love.

Honor All

Honor is the currency of the Kingdom of God. Every single human being on the planet was created by God. And even if people rub you the wrong way, you can choose to honor all anyway. Anchor your heart in that commitment. When you want to gossip or talk about someone else, you will remember it. It guards your heart from indulging in bitterness. It guards your mouth from saying hurtful things. It guards what you do, and it guards your integrity. It helps you to follow through on your promises. Choosing to honor the people in your life changes the way you do life with them.

When I first started living my life full out for Jesus, my parents didn't agree with some of the decisions that I made. When I stepped into business, some of my friends questioned my focus on money, and even my salvation because of it. I was a financial coach, it's difficult to be one, and not talk about money and its impact on people's lives. If I hadn't been guided by honor, it would have been easy to burn some of those relationships. But then, I would have lost the accountability, the rich community, and the people that God had surrounded me with that helped me walk that journey.

Honoring others doesn't mean that you will always agree. It also doesn't mean that you let other people control the decisions you make. But it will inform the way that you have those conversations. Even during times of tension, you'll speak with humility, putting the needs of others above yourself, while also remaining firmly planted in God's calling. Operating with a heart of humility and honor means you can also acknowledge that you're not always right. You're quick to apologize if you're wrong. You're quick to call yourself out, before you call anyone else out.

Jesus' famous "sermon on the mount" in Matthew 5-7 provides many guiding principles on how to live with other believers. The core of that sermon is that Jesus' commanded us to live with humility, and honor others. To honor others in such a way that you're showing people they matter, they belong, can be a part of the community, whether that's a ministry community, a business community, or community in some other context. These principles can help create authentic, healthy, God-honoring togetherness.

Worship Is A Lifestyle

Worship is the culmination of everything you do. Worship is that moment where you are beyond tired from a long day at work, you come home, your child is acting like they have no manners, and everything in you wants to snap at them. Instead of responding with frustration and anger, you worship God by exercising patience while you address what needs to be addressed.

Worship is doing a business deal and noticing that a client overpays by a thousand dollars, and saying, "Hey, you overpaid me. Here's your thousand dollars back." Worship is playing cards with your family, knowing all you have to do is lie in order to win, and deciding not to because it's not worth it. Worship is wanting to say something unkind – even if true – about someone else but holding your tongue and checking your heart. Worship is seeking to honor God in every moment of your life.

Avoid the Opportunity Trap

When you start taking action, doors will often start to open. People will start offering you opportunities because they see you can get things done. When that happens, you need to reflect on your ultimate objective, your calling, and limit the number of things you do. There will always be needs, but you are not called to meet every single one. You must be moved by God's leadership, and not people's needs otherwise things will go sideways very quickly.

When it felt like I was doing many things for a lot of people in ministry, my dad said to me, "Toyin, there will always be ministry. But if you work yourself into the ground, you're going to die. And there's still going to be more ministry work to do. Put a limit on what you do, so that you stay alive long enough to be effective in any one thing." The same is true for you.

Stop Caring What Others Think

You need to be fully aware of your current season, and your primary focus in that season. Make decisions that support and align with the season you're in, and that are consistent with what you've been called to.

I see too many people trying to obey God while at the same time trying to keep up with the Joneses. They feel the need to have everything perfectly balanced, house perfectly kept, pray 3 hours a day, volunteer on the weekends, work 40 hours a week plus homeschool and of course have all the frills they see others have around them. That is the recipe for disaster. I have found that it is much easier to know exactly what God has asked me to prioritize in a season, focus on that and let go of the small stuff.

For example, I do not feel upset when my house is dirty or messy, because I understand that when you have toddlers (which I currently do), their full-time job is creating messes - if you've ever tried sorting laundry with a toddler assistant you know what I mean. You fix it as you can, but focus on enjoying your current season. There will come a time when they will be adults and gone, your house will be pristine, but did you fully enjoy them while you had them?

I used to pray for hours a day when I was single and in fulltime ministry, and that availability in my schedule changed with diapers, dishes and the business to run. I remember when God encouraged me that He could meet with and speak to me just as easily while I do the dishes as when I would sit in the House of Prayer for hours. Understand your current season and do the best job you can, to be the reflection of Jesus there. Remain flexible, and listen for when God wants to change your focus.

God's Grace For Your Action

God is amazing. He is willing to direct us step by step. At every crossroad we get to, He is willing to tell us which way to go, as long as we move. You may have external displays of your affections to Jesus in the place of prayer, but are you willing to put your action behind it? The biggest question He has for you when everyone goes home and your phone's camera is off, is, "Are you willing to do what I am asking you to do? Do you love me enough to obey me with your life?"

God has called us to be the answer to our own prayers, the answer to the issues in this world. Almost all of the stories of obedience I share in this book were birthed in the place of prayer.

So don't sit still on your prayers. Will Rogers once said, "If you're on the right track, but you sit there long enough, eventually you will get run over." If you know what God is calling you to do, take action and do it. Opportunities do pass and the timing of God's call matters. So, if you know what God is saying, step out. Step into it. Trust God with the outcome. And then, make the next decision.

I began this book by sharing my journey about how I used to think God was a boring taskmaster that only cared about whether or not we followed the rules. I believed that holiness was simply a list of do's and don'ts.

But God's call to holiness and consecration isn't just for the sake of obedience, it is *for you.* My entire life changed when I stopped fighting to see how close I could get to sin while remaining in Christ, and started pushing for how close I could get to Him. Paul said, "I strictly discipline my body and make it my slave, so that, after I have preached to others, I myself will not be disqualified." I pray for you that you will not be disqualified. That you will be open for Abba to speak to your heart in whatever area He chooses, and that you would be transformed into His image from glory to glory.

When you surrender to God and fully live for Him, you're transformed. And in that transformation, you start experiencing life on a whole different level. You experience a passion, purpose, and power that you never thought possible.

ACTIVATION POINTS

- What barriers do you think hinders people from experiencing the fullness of God's presence in their lives?
- Reflect on the significance of Jesus' death and resurrection in granting us access to God. How does knowing that Jesus has won you access to a relationship with God inspire you in your daily life?
- How intentional are you in seeking God's presence and guidance in your life? What steps can you take to deepen your relationship with God on a daily basis?
- How can you cultivate a lifestyle of bold faith in your prayer life?
- Reflect on instances where you've found yourself complaining rather than being thankful. How can you shift your focus from complaining to gratitude? How can

you cultivate a spirit of joy-filled surrender?

- In what areas is God challenging you to live differently from the world? How can you honor Him by living a consecrated life in those areas?
- How do you view the role of community and accountability in your spiritual walk? What changes can you make to become more actively engaged in a supportive Christian community?
- Consider your typical day. How can you invite the Holy Spirit to work through you in your daily activities? What steps can you take to operate in the gifts of the Holy Spirit more intentionally in this season of your life?
- How can you prioritize rest and rejuvenation in your life? How does your understanding of rest reflect your trust in God's provision and sovereignty?
- Plan a Sabbath day for yourself and your family. How can you make this time separate and focused on God?
- Choose one person in your life whom you find challenging to honor. How can you intentionally demonstrate honor towards them?
- Reflect on the opportunities currently presented to you. Do they align with your ultimate objectives and calling? How can you adapt your schedule to honor your current season?
- Identify one area in your life where you feel pressured to conform to societal expectations. How can you prioritize God's calling over people's opinions?

- Reflect on the opportunities currently presented to you. Do they align with your ultimate objectives and calling? How can you adapt your schedule to honor your current season?
- Identify one area in your life where you feel pressured to conform to societal expectations. How can you prioritize God's calling over people's opinions?

SURPRISE!

In true Toyin fashion, I have a surprise for you!

As I wrote this book, I was in the middle of another faith journey. One day at church while I was worshipping God, I received a chorus that encouraged me tremendously to believe that God would come through on His word. I decided to turn that chorus into a song to be shared with you, my reader.

And of course, despite the fact that God had called me out of songwriting/music for 9 years, despite the fact that I had never done a music video at the level He asked me to execute with only 4 days to plan and film... His Spirit and heart rested on the song and video, and caused it to go viral with over 450,000 worshippers joining us to sing about the faithfulness of God.

This song is a declaration of faith in a God who can do what looks impossible. This is for those of you who are in a place of obedience and believing for a breakthrough you do not yet see.

It is called *"What Is Too Difficult For You" by Toyin Crandell* and is an accompaniment to this book. It is free to access on Spotify, Apple Music, YouTube, and anywhere else you access music.

Go listen to it right now. I know it will bless you!

CONCLUSION

Before I wrap up this book, I will share the tremendous blessings I have seen from following Abba in wholehearted obedience. He took me from totally unsaved and living for myself to truly finding joy in living for and following Him. I was stuck in sin with no idea how to break out of that cycle, and stuck in an unhealthy relationship that I kept running back to. He transformed my heart, and my life. He promised me in Ezekiel 36 that He would take out my heart of stone and give me a heart of flesh, and that's exactly what He did.

I've had so many adventures with God. He's had me:

- Lead teams of young adults to Parliament Hill to discuss issues that matter to young Canadians.
- Write, record and release four albums and win an award for best female gospel artist while I was in full-time music ministry.
- Spend 9 years working in the social sector; I've been an Assistant Director for a system of 27 shelters, for men coming out of addiction.
- Spend 15 years in ministry: worship leading, teaching, and 3 years of street ministry assisting the homeless. I've toured across Ontario ministering in song, spoken word, and preaching and seeing the gospel come to life!
- Tour across Canada training Christians on how to engage with the government positively.

- Travel to Cambodia to serve women living in the slums; showing them how treasured and valuable they are.
- Run for political office and become one of the only young black women as a Federal candidate for one of the major political parties.
- Coach other government officials to win political campaigns and get into municipal, and federal office successfully.
- Run a media production company that released 4 albums, published two bestselling books and organized a Flashmob in the Pan Am Games all within one year.
- Led us out of our tiny Toronto basement apartment, 3 hours away from everything that was familiar to us, which enabled the purchase our first home miraculously. That became the foundation for all our other real estate purchases.
-
- Following Him in business which led to:
- 11 streams of income.
- Multiple real estate properties.
- Running a multimillion dollar company.
- Celebrating our clients paying off millions of dollars of debt, becoming multimillionaires themselves in record time, and gaining the freedom they dreamed of.
- Going from reading SUCCESS Magazine at the age of 16, to becoming a winner of the SUCCESS 2023 Women of Influence Awards

- CEO of the 74th fastest growing company in Canada according to the Globe and Mail with a verified 592% growth in 3 years.
- National Television Show co-host for a show featured on 9 networks.

But more than all these, obedience has led my family and I to develop quality friendships all over the world with people who truly add so much value to others. It was these friendships that allowed me to record and produce the song and music video, within 3 weeks of deciding to add that as a bonus to this book - after not producing music for years. I'm blessed to have done all of this by the age of 35! Wow! Obedience is your gift to Abba, and it is Abba's gift to you! Don't miss out on the journey.

Now, one final story. Sometimes God will ask you to do something well out of the ordinary. In running my business I had gotten into a rhythm. We had a strong marketing strategy that produced consistent leads and I didn't need to change anything. One day, He highlighted to me that we had only one strong marketing strategy, and it was time to diversify how we got clients.

It was one of the highest pressure moments in the company, with a major transition that had taken place, and just after having my third baby. He told me to think bigger than I previously had. Even though our company had only done a few million in revenue per year up to that point, I decided that we would have a million dollars in sales in one week.

I was so used to checking in with people that I automatically let a few business mentors know. It was not well received. Holy Spirit said, come and let Me show you. He led me to have two conversations with friends of mine, and put together a funnel that I had not seen before that point. It was a combination of the online business evergreen, challenge, and joint venture models. We took 2 weeks to build all the technology and automation (which we had never done before), and had only 7 days to advertise. The business ended up earning over $1,200,000 in a week and a half. I was blown away.

I could share so many other stories of God's amazing demonstration of power, but enough about me—

It's Your Turn!

In Part One of this book, I explained the foundation for our obedience, which is understanding the immense love that God has shown toward us in the work of the cross. Simply put, when you are aware of how much you've been forgiven and set free from, there is nothing too big to do in our response to God.

We examined the lies and habits that often stop us from obeying, even when we want to. We addressed the necessity for developing muscles of perseverance, faith, and resilience, whether we feel like things are happening the way we expected them or not.

We explored the foundation of obedience in God's love language, and His expectation for us to obey if we say that we are His friends. This is possible, whether you are a missionary, stay at home mom, or working a full-time job.

In Part Two of this book, we addressed the practical steps for obedience. We discussed how to develop habits of obedience rather than disobedience. We explored how to hear God's voice and determine the timing of what He is asking you to do. We also discussed how to build trust in Him in the midst of the challenges as you step out in faith, and what to do when it feels like you fell flat on your face. I hope you spent time reviewing that section to examine your heart and see whether you are currently developing habits of obedience. I challenge you to complete the activation points and practice these principles.

In Part Three we discussed the power of prayer, and the power of the Holy Spirit as we obey. He empowers us to follow God's will and enables us to do what we could not accomplish in our own strength.

So what do you need to obey? You need a genuine connection and relationship with God. You need to get into His word, but more than anything, you need to begin to take those steps of faith and practice following right here, right now. These shifts alone are enough to propel you into consistency in building a history with God.

Now you have a choice. You can either take all the information I've just given you and forget all about it. Or, you can begin the journey of faith and expand. You can learn how to build those muscles of faith, courage, self-awareness, and discipline.

Here's How We Can Help

As I mentioned, many people have invested their wisdom and time into my success, and I am committed to doing the same for others. Our vision is a world where success is defined not just by wealth, but by freedom, well-being, and the positive impact you create. Now, I know that there are others who are exactly where I used to be. You are hungry for change. You will do whatever that requires of you with integrity and morality. You are ready to walk this journey out with the Lord, and to do so in a community that helps you to stay accountable to your commitments. While others are willing to settle for the Sunday-to-Sunday Christianity, you know that is not your life. You want to know your life was spent honouring God at the highest levels possible.

You know that it's not comfortable to change the trajectory of your life from stuck, mediocre, and "just getting by," to a life with a legacy. You want to give the generations to come something to be grateful for from your journey.

We have multiple classes, retreats, and two primary programs through which we walk with those who are committed to their change in a focused way. By the grace of God, I have been able to assist thousands in walking into their shift whether financial, or in their journey of self-mastery.

I invite you to visit www.SelfMasteryAcademy.ca if you would like to join this community. In this room we focus on helping you develop the practical habits that aid your desire to obey. Habits like mental toughness, resilience, courage and the ability to make decisions quickly, so that you are able to run without regret. Visit the website to learn more about the programs available in the Academy. You can join immediately or down the road, either way we would love to have you in the Mastery Room.

If you are looking for a financial shift, I invite you to visit www.MoneyMindsetShift.ca, and join my next free online masterclass. At the end of it, I will share a link through which you can book a call with a member of my team, so that we can speak to you personally about applying these principles to your mind, and to your finances starting today. Whatever your biggest challenges are, we've seen them, and we know how to overcome them.

If we are a fit you may be invited into our 8-week program, *Money Mindset SHIFT.* This is where we help people shift into the fullness of God's purpose for their business, career, and overall finances. Every single person who has been through our program has identified it as a moment of change in their lives. If we are not a fit, you will receive personalized recommendations for what your next steps should be.

Finally, I'll say this, people are rewarded in public for what they have practiced for years in private. Stop focusing on your image and begin focusing on your change today.

I would like to personally congratulate you for choosing to prioritize your journey with the Lord by investing in yourself, reading, and applying the lessons from this book. I pray that God's perfect will for your life is established, and that you prosper in all things as your soul prospers.

To your freedom in Christ,
Toyin Crandell
www.ToyinCrandell.com

PSALM 128

Happy are those who obey the Lord,
who live by his commands.

Your work will provide for your needs;
 you will be happy and prosperous.
Your wife will be like a fruitful vine in your home,
and your children will be like young olive trees around your table.
A man who obeys the Lord
will surely be blessed like this.
May the Lord bless you from Zion!
May you see Jerusalem prosper
all the days of your life!
May you live to see your grandchildren!

Peace be with Israel!

ACKNOWLEDGEMENTS

Thank you to my husband, Joshua Crandell, for your patience and support over these 8 years of envisioning and working on this book. Thank you for your consistent encouragement. Thank you to my 3 children, Maranatha, Nehemiah and Esperanza Crandell, I love and am deeply grateful for you.

Thank you to my parents, Pastor Amos and Eyitayo Dada, and Tim and Carol Crandell who prayed for me through this wild rollercoaster of a journey. Who have stood in the gap for more people than I can imagine, and whose commitment to the Lord is evident both in public and in private.

Thank you to my four sisters, two sisters-in-law, and three brothers-in-law –Dara and Ade, Ife, Tobi, Debbie, Jason and Melissa, Nick and Vicky – and the many children we've been blessed with. What a blessing it is to be a part of such a large, joyful, and unified family!

Thank you to the Jeremiah House Publishing team for your help converting my lived experience and many speaking engagements into a beautifully crafted, published book.

Thank you to Chris-Ann Manning for capturing my voice and for your excellent work copy and content editing this project. You are a gift and a friend.

Thank you to Tracy Havens for your assistance copy editing this project as well.

Thank you to every single person who prayed me through this writing process, it was a wild one, but we got it done!

I believe that many people will shift from the boring, mundane expression of faith into a fuller expression of their passion for Jesus because of your collective efforts.

God bless you family.

ABOUT THE AUTHOR

Toyin Crandell, bestselling author of *Money Mindset SHIFT.*, a ministry leader and financial coach, brings a wealth of diverse experiences to the conversation on radical obedience to God. With a background in biology from York University, Toyin's journey of faith took her:

- From living a fake, hypocritical lifestyle, to a radical lover of Jesus Christ.
- From being spat on while street-preaching, to a federal political candidate.
- From homeless and without food, to a multi-millionaire in 3 years.
- From business, back to daily prayer groups and bible study.

As a worship leader and recording artist with 4 albums, the former CEO of a successful media production company, and current CEO of the 74th fastest growing company in Canada, Toyin's life shows **what God can do with a life that is fully surrendered to Him.** Her coaching platforms have impacted over 50,000 people, guiding them towards financial freedom and personal mastery.

Toyin combines compelling storytelling with down to earth, practical insights, to help you **embrace obedience in your own life so you have a rich personal history with God.**

Book Toyin as a Keynote Speaker for your next live or virtual event, or podcast, visit www.ToyinCrandell.com

Other Titles From Jeremiah House Publishing

Available on Amazon, Indigo, Barnes and Nobles and wherever books are sold

Money Mindset SHIFT. Church Edition: The Top 9 Myths That Keep Christians Stuck Financially and How To Get Unstuck, Live Debt Free and Build Wealth!

If you have ever prayed for financial breakthrough and waited... and waited, only to be disappointed, you are not alone. Millions of Christians are working hard, trying to provide for their families and leave a legacy for their children's children but are finding themselves stuck in lack, or having just enough to get by.

If you have ever felt like there was an elephant in the room at church: no one wants to admit how frustrated they feel financially but everyone is always "blessed and highly favoured"...

If you see clear financial patterns you've tried to break out of but keep returning to...

If you have achieved a fair level of success in your career but feel like you have plateaued...

If you love to give and support people and ministries in need, but don't have the means to give at the level you desire... This book is for you.

In *Money Mindset SHIFT. Church Edition*, high-performance mindset, and finance coach Toyin Crandell sets out to assist Christians called to the marketplace through their career or business.

She identifies the top 9 myths specific to Christians that keep them stuck financially, and gives practical wisdom for getting unstuck, living debt free and building wealth so they can leave a legacy for generations to come, to the glory of God.

Your journey to being a financial pillar for your family, community, ministries, and missionaries while having a vibrant relationship with God through His Son, Jesus Christ begins *now*.

The Squirrel and The Oak Tree - Joshua Crandell

The Squirrel & The Oak Tree is a Canadian folk tale that helps children ages 4-8 learn about values like trust, openness and how to overcome stereotypes and develop friendships with people who are different. Join a quick-tempered squirrel and a wise old crow as they discover an uncommon friendship and learn that: "Things are not always what they seem to be, and sometimes we miss what others can see."

Making Your Marriage Work, Maama's Practical Wisdom For A Lasting, Happy Marriage - Eyitayo Dada

Marriage is not meant to be endured, it is meant to be enjoyed. Too many couples are either bored or holding on "for God's sake" or "for the sake of their children". With practical advice based in the word of God, this book will help revive the joy, passion and laughter in your marriage

Lily Among Thorns - Mia Christine

Lily among thorns gives creative guidance to finding contentment in a world of never enough. For every heart overwhelmed with disappointment, difficulty and the uncertainty of life, these poems, songs, and short stories trumpet bold statements for resilient living, leading the unsatisfied into lasting joy and freedom.

Awaken My Heart: Listening For
The Still Small Voice - Julia McDonald

Follow Julia on her journey through the Psalms and Proverbs, as she shares lessons from her personal devotionals and then, begin your own! Fill the pages with your own prayers and insights as you search for God in the scriptures. Today is the day for your heart to be awakened to a more intimate relationship with God!

Albums Featuring Toyin Crandell

Available on iTunes, Spotify and CDBaby

What Is Too Difficult For You - Toyin Crandell [Single]

A passionate worship song declaring God's faithfulness and omnipotence. There is nothing too difficult for our God to do. The intercessor's worship soundtrack.

Declaration of Dependence - Toyin Crandell

Resonating with soul/jazz vocals and blues-gospel influences, "Declaration of Dependence" gives voice to the dark night of the soul - where God's presence and promises seem most distant - while revealing the comfort, joy and strength found in Christ.

Broken Spirit, Contrite Heart - Toyin Dada

The devoted, the disillusioned and everyone in between converge at the fundamental desire to experience true, pure love. "Broken Spirit, Contrite Heart" is that access point between listener and the personhood of Jesus Christ, unveiling the beauty and depth of His love - a worship experience both refreshing and liberating for any individual with an open ear.

Sparrow - Joshua Crandell

Sparrow's unique blend of R&B, easy listening and jazz highlights encourages listeners to live in patience, peace, and confident trust in the faithfulness of God.

Living Out Love - The Love Movement 4:16

Living Out Love captures the journey of following Jesus Christ through a dynamic mix of soothing acoustic rhythms and catchy electro pop riffs. Jesus' life example ignites our hearts to respond in radical love, faith, and obedience.

Love Letters - Toyin Dada

With its multi-generational sounds and distinctive vocals, Toyin Dada's debut album "Love Letters' succeeds in capturing the unique dynamics of the love relationship between a fiery God and His beloved creation.

Additional Recommended Reading
These are books that have strengthened my faith in addition to the Word of God.

- Rees Howells Intercessor - Norman Grubb
- The Bait of Satan - John Bevere
- Anointed For Business - Ed Silvoso
- Money Mindset SHIFT. - Toyin Crandell
- They Shall Expel Demons - Derek Prince
- Driven By Eternity - John Bevere
- Radical Obedience - Toyin Crandell
- Practicing the Presence of God - Brother Lawrence
- Why Revival Tarries - Leanoard Ravenhill
- The Heavenly Man - Brother Yun
- Dream Dreams and Have Dominion - Dr. Amos Dada
- Marked - Faytene Grasseschi
- The Fourth Dimension - Dr. David Yonggi Cho
- A Tale of Three Kings - Gene Edwards
- Making Your Marriage Work - Eyitayo Dada
- Dealing With The Rejection and Praise of Man - Bob Sorge
- The Knowledge of the Holy - A. W. Tozer
- When Heaven Invades Earth - Bill Johnson
- Healthy and Free - Beni Johnson

Visit http://toyincrandell.com/lifehacks for more resources

Made in the USA
Middletown, DE
11 October 2024

62450661R00161